MW01711205

SASKATOON PIE!

Geoffrey Ursell

COTEAU BOOKS

To Barbara with Love

Cover photograph R-B674 courtesy of the Saskatchewan Archives Board.
Cover and book design by Duncan Campbell.
Printed and bound in Canada.

The author wishes to thank the Canada Council, the Globe Theatre, Kim McCaw, Victor A. Young, and Tibor Feheregyhazi for their assistance in the development of this play.

Canadian Cataloguing in Publication Data

Ursell, Geoffrey
Saskatoon pie!
(Florence James series ; 3)
A play.
ISBN 1-55050-044-9
1. Saskatchewan - History - Drama. I. Title.
II. Series.
PS8591.R73S37 1993 C812' .54 C93-098021-2
PR9199.3.U74S37 1993

COTEAU BOOKS
401-2206 Dewdney Ave.
Regina, Saskatchewan
Canada S4R 1H3

AVAILABLE IN THE US FROM
General Distribution Services
4500 Witmer Industrial Estates
Niagara Falls, NY, 14305-1386

The publisher gratefully acknowledges the financial assistance of the Saskatchewan Arts Board, the Canada Council for the Arts, the Government of Canada through the Book Publishing Industry Development Program (BPIDP), and the City of Regina Arts Commission, for its publishing program.

The Canada Council for the Arts
Le Conseil des Arts du Canada
SASKATCHEWAN ARTS BOARD
Canada
City of Regina

FOREWORD

THE ORIGINAL PRODUCTION OF *Saskatoon Pie!* TOOK PLACE AT SASKATOON'S Persephone Theatre a couple of years before I moved to Saskatchewan. I was later able to see a remounted version that toured the province in 1986. It was an energetic and loving piece of theatre, performed with terrific eccentricities and side-splitting humour. The audience was charmed, watching egos colliding in the process of a "proper" and "correct" European culture being imposed upon the "Wild West" of Saskatchewan.

Saskatoon Pie! captured the voices and examined the personal agendas of those who wished to "develop" the "Land of Promise." Throughout the play, Geoffrey Ursell poked fun at the kinds of social structures and bureaucrats that emerge with frightening suddenness when a new order is being imposed. *Saskatoon Pie!* was a major hit both in Saskatoon and across the province. Audiences loved its gentle yet barbed retelling of local legends.

The play follows the traditional style of a two-act musical comedy, with uncluttered and uplifting songs. It successfully grabs the attention of the audience as they recognize the age-old struggle between Justice and Corruption. The cheering on of the "good guys" (in this case, the women); the clarity of the characters and their relationships; and the good-natured humour gives us a lot to laugh at and to celebrate in this entertaining, all-Saskatchewan musical comedy.

For above all else, *Saskatoon Pie!* gives us the opportunity to laugh at ourselves, at our naiveté and single-mindedness. With obvious love and tremendous respect for the province, Geoffrey Ursell captures in the play the energy and spirit that make Saskatchewan original, perverse, harsh, and still full of generosity. Geoffrey's political voice is strong. With humour, with lyrics, with music, he tells us that Good will prevail and the Corrupt will eventually fail – or at least be made to compromise!

TOM BENTLEY-FISHER
Artistic Director
Twenty-Fifth Street Theatre

PREFACE

THE HISTORY OF *Saskatoon Pie!* WITH PERSEPHONE THEATRE HAS BEEN A joyous experience for me. First of all, the play won the theatre's national playwriting competition in 1981, and was produced in the spring of the following year. The theatre was in trouble; the artistic director had just resigned. But Victor Young directed a sparkling production, and the play took off – performances sold out, and the run was extended by a week. Four years later, Tibor Feheregyhazi, who had taken over as artistic director in 1981 and had seen the first production, remounted the play, and again audiences packed the theatre. And then, for the following month, they filled high school gyms and church halls across the province, as *Saskatoon Pie!* went on tour. It was especially pleasing for me to see a performance of the play in a sold-out large church hall in Regina – where it's set – and hear the knowledgeable laughter at all the local jokes.

I'd begun working on what was to become the play sometime early in 1979 with the assistance of the Canada Council. One of the first elements was the song "Saskatoon Pie," co-written with my wife and fellow writer, Barbara Sapergia. Later that year, Globe Theatre gave me a commission to complete the play and provided a workshop in May of 1980, directed by Kim McCaw.

I wanted to write in the form of a musical comedy, but I also wanted to deal with some serious questions. The workshop revealed how difficult it was to put too much pressure on the form, and clarified the final shape of the play.

Growing up in Regina, I'd always been impressed by the size of the provincial legislature, which, it was claimed, "possesses the longest continuous corridor of any legislature building in the British Commonwealth." And when you're a kid, everyone knows, such things look even bigger than they really are. What I didn't know then, and what the research of a friend, Don Humphries, revealed to me, was what scandal surrounded the purchase of the land for that building. The possibility of political corruption – perfect material for satire.

At the same time, women were fighting for the vote. Why not, I wondered, have an untested Nellie McClung, known in the play by her other name, Letitia, make a visit as a guest speaker? She's there at the invitation of Anya Burke, mother of Natasha, who is working as a maid in Mayor Raker's home.

Throw in the young investigative reporter, Percy Thistle, who loves Alice Raker. And finally, an operetta they're all going to do as a command Dominion Day performance for Premier Scott and the members of the legislature, who are trying to decide whether Saskatoon, Moose Jaw, or Regina will become the capital of the province.

Add a piano player. And some songs.

There is a serious underpinning to all of the comic plots, counterplots, and lampooning of the CPR, lawyers, and politicians. The patriarchical structure of power in 1906 society is made very evident in the play. And, by the end, it is at least symbolically overthrown and forced to make some accommodation with the collective power of the women. It's clear, as well, that Percy, who has been somewhat corrupted by his involvement with the patriarchy, must learn new ways of behaving. Nonetheless, the power the men have is not going to be surrendered easily or without an ongoing fight.

I hoped that, in the midst of all the laughter at Mayor Raker, Mr. Shrike, Mr. Ink, and Percy appearing in the operetta dressed as women, some questions about the nature of male and female roles, some questions about who has power and why, popped into the minds of the people watching.

And will, in future productions, pop again.

Saskatoon Pie! had its premiere at Persephone Theatre, April 30, 1982 with the following cast:

NATASHA BURKE	Andorlie Hillstrom
PERCY THISTLE	David Talbot
ALICE RAKER	Cheryl Stilling
ANYA BURKE	Helen Beavis
MAYOR SIDNEY RAKER	Gabriel Prendergast
MR. SHRIKE	Wilfrid Dube
MR. INK	Michael Bianchin
JEAN	Kate Pierpoint
LETITIA M^C^CLUNG	Marlane O'Brien
PIANO PLAYER	Lloyd Nicholson

DIRECTOR	Victor A. Young
SET DESIGN	John Ferguson
COATUMES	Marie-Lousie Wittlin
LIGHTING	Jim McManamy
MUSICAL DIRECTION AND ARRANGEMENTS	Lloyd Nicholson
STAGE MANAGER	Rick Gorrie

CHARACTERS
(in order of appearance)

PIANO PLAYER

NATASHA: *Daughter of Anya. A maid in the Mayor's house.*

PERCY THISTLE: *A young reporter for* The Leader. *From Saskatoon.*

MISS ALICE RAKER: *Daughter of the Mayor.*

MRS. ANYA BURKE *A cleaning woman at the CPR station. Ukrainian. A member of the Women's Labour League.*

MR. SIDNEY RAKER: *Mayor of Regina.*

MR. SHRIKE: *A CPR executive. Of British descent. A dandy.*

MR. INK: *A lawyer. An alcoholic.*

JEAN: *Secretary to Ink. Scottish. A member of the Womens' Christian Temperance Union.*

LETITIA: *A guest speaker for the Suffrage meeting.*

SONGS

ACT ONE

"When You're Working on a Paper" PERCY, ALICE, NATASHA
"We're the Ones" RAKER, SHRIKE, INK
"Saskatoon Pie" ALICE, PERCY
"Demon Drink!" JEAN, ANYA, LETITIA
"Hot Prairie Sun" ALICE, NATASHA
"Booze!" RAKER, SHRIKE, INK
"A Clever, Clever Trick" RAKER, SHRIKE, INK, PERCY

ACT TWO

"We Are Marching" ANYA, JEAN, NATASHA, LETITIA
"The Vote" ALL
"Men, Men, Men" RAKER, SHRIKE, INK, PERCY
"Never Seek" ALICE, ANYA, NATASHA
"When I Fall Asleep" ALICE, PERCY

The Operetta
"Magic Reversals Waltz" RAKER, SHRIKE, INK, ANYA, JEAN
"Love (Times 9) Song" PERCY, NATASHA, RAKER, SHRIKE, INK, ANYA, JEAN
"Revolution" RAKER, SHRIKE, INK, PERCY

"Saskatoon Pie" (Reprise) ALL

ACT ONE

Scene One

Dominion Day, 1906, Regina, Saskatchewan

The PIANO PLAYER *plays the Overture.*

Lights rise. Early morning. The MAYOR'S *house. There is a front entrance, a door to the hall leading to the study and the bedrooms, and a door to the hall leading to the kitchen. By the entrance door is an umbrella stand filled with umbrellas, parasols, walking sticks, and a feather duster. There is a sideboard, with bottles of liquor inside.* NATASHA *opens the door and lets* PERCY THISTLE *in. He has a monogrammed handkerchief in his jacket pocket. He carries a newspaper.*

NATASHA: Why Mr. Thistle!

PERCY: Good morning, Natasha, you're looking very lovely this morning.

NATASHA: Thank you, Mr. Thistle.

PERCY: Now, I've told you to call me Percy. Isn't it a wonderful morning? Do you know that the birds started to sing at exactly 3:33 A.M.? Right after the passenger train arrived. The whistle blew, and all of a sudden the air was filled with beautiful music! Is Alice awake yet? I bet she isn't! Is the Mayor in his study? Is there any breakfast on?

NATASHA *(during this):* I...really...I....

ALICE *enters from the hall to the bedrooms and the study.*

ALICE: Percy!

PERCY: Alice! *(He whirls her off her feet and they kiss.)*

ALICE *(laughing):* What are you doing here at this hour? I thought you never got out of bed until noon!

PERCY: I never went to bed.

ALICE: You couldn't sleep?

PERCY: For thinking about you.

ALICE: Oh, Percy! *(Laughs.)* Have you had breakfast?

PERCY: No, just fifty cups of strong tea.

ALICE *(to* NATASHA) Natasha, fix another place for Mr. Thistle.

NATASHA: Yes, miss. *(She exits.* PERCY *watches her go.)*

ALICE: Now, what have you really been doing? *(She adjusts his handkerchief, recalling his attention.)*

Music for "When You're Working on a Paper" begins.

PERCY *(hands over paper):* Here it is! The Special Edition for Dominion Day. I've been working on it all night.

ALICE: A special edition of *The Leader!*

PERCY *(begins song, talking, then singing as song gets faster):*

I've had to put this Special Issue all together by myself
Had to read a ton of papers that were piled upon the shelf
Had to write two dozen stories on our past and present glories
And leave out all the things you shouldn't tell!

ALICE *wags finger.*

NATASHA *re-enters during the following.*

PERCY: First the editor –

ALICE: Our Premier –

PERCY: – saw me yesterday at six.

He came running in the office and said, "We're in a fix!
Dominion Day's tomorrow, you can beg or steal or borrow
But I want some stories, and I want them quick!"

ALICE & NATASHA:

Right quick!
Dominion Day's tomorrow, you can beg or steal or borrow
But I want some stories

ALL: And I want them quick!

PERCY:

“So take a look at all our history, but don’t be too complete
When you’re looking back at history, you have to be discreet
We have a society who don’t want notoriety
For things that may have taken place last week!”

ALICE & NATASHA:

We have a society who don’t want notoriety
For things that may have taken place last week!

PERCY *(chorus):*

When you’re working on a paper you can never get a rest!
When you’re working on a paper, you just have to do your best!

ALICE & NATASHA:

When you’re working on a paper you can never get a rest!
When you’re working on a paper, you just have to do your best!

NATASHA: Your best!

ALICE: Your best!

PERCY: Your best! *(End chorus.)*

PERCY *(faster):*

I did a story on the buffalo, a story on their bones
A story on how Edgar Dewdney found us all this home
And the tracks and railway station that both link us to the nation
And the winter we had ninety feet of snow!

ALICE: Percy, no!

PERCY:

I describe Inauguration Day, nineteen oh five
When we first became a Province, oh our happiness and pride
And the splendid decorations and the festive celebrations
And the Mounties and their music –

ALICE: And their famous ride!

ALICE & NATASHA:

And the splendid decorations and the festive celebrations
And the Mounties

ALL: And their music, and their ride!

PERCY:

I did a story on Regina, and one more on Saskatoon
And on how the Legislature will convene this afternoon
To decide which population will be filled with jubilation
And which of them *(voice going down)* will have to face its doom!

ALICE & NATASHA *(also low voice):* Its doom!

ALL:

To decide which population will be filled with jubilation
And which of them will have to face its doom!

Now PERCY *repeats the verse about the buffalo, while* ALICE *does the verse about Inauguration Day, and* NATASHA *does the verse about Regina and Saskatoon – all at the same time. Then* PERCY *sings the chorus through once, and* ALICE *and* NATASHA *join the second time through.*

PERCY *(faster yet):*

So I've been working all the night and I couldn't stop for sleep
And I couldn't stop to think and I couldn't stop to eat
And the copy was aflowing and the presses started rolling
And at last this Special Issue hit the street!

ALICE & NATASHA: The street!

ALL now launch into the chorus, which ends with seven alternating "Your best!"s and a collapse into laughter.

NATASHA: Breakfast is ready.

ALICE: Thank you, Natasha.

PERCY: I hope it's something special...I'm starved.

NATASHA: Our meals are always special when you're here.

ALICE *gives* NATASHA *a look and takes* PERCY*'s arm.*

ALICE: May I have the pleasure, Mr. Thistle?

PERCY: Of course, Miss Raker.

They start to go off and there is a knock at the door. PERCY *and* ALICE *exit.* NATASHA *goes to the entrance door. She lets in* ANYA. *She carries a roll of posters.*

NATASHA: Mother, what are you doing here?

ANYA: I forgot to tell you to ask Mr. Teesol to our meeting.

NATASHA: He's here right now.

ANYA*(looks around):* That is fine.

NATASHA: And you're going to finish putting up the posters?

ANYA: With Jean. She's got the brush and glue.

NATASHA: It's a good thing you don't have to work today.

ANYA: I'll have twice as much to do to get the station clean tomorrow, but even the CPR has to let some of its workers have today as a holiday.

RAKER *coughs offstage.*

NATASHA: I'd better go prepare breakfast for the Mayor.

RAKER*(off):* Natasha?

NATASHA: Yes, sir?

RAKER: Is breakfast – *(He enters, sees* ANYA*. He knows who she is, but pretends he doesn't.)* Oh…and who is this?

NATASHA: This is my mother, sir.

RAKER: Your mother…Mrs.….

ANYA*(showing deference):* My name is Mrs. Burke. Anya Burke.

RAKER: I'm pleased to meet you, Mrs. Burke. *(To* NATASHA.) Why don't you get the breakfast ready? I'll see your mother to the door.

NATASHA: Right away, sir.

She exits. RAKER *waits for her to leave.*

RAKER*(under breath):* You agreed never to come here…never. What do you want?

ANYA: Nothing very much, Mr. Mayor. I only want you to come to our meeting at noon.

RAKER: Your meeting? You already sent an invitation to my office about that.

ANYA: Yes, I did. But it is a very important meeting for the women of this city. We've brought a speaker all the way from Winnipeg, and I want you to say a few words of welcome.

RAKER: And you didn't think I'd show up at a Suffrage meeting.

ANYA: No, I didn't. But you will now, won't you?

RAKER: I don't know if I can fit it in. I've got a lot of meetings today. The Legislature....

ANYA: Yes, I know they're all in town. But this meeting is only across the street...in the park.

RAKER: If you keep your promise never to come to this house again.

ANYA: Things can't go on like this forever, you know.

RAKER: I don't see why not.

ANYA: They have to know, sooner or later.

There is a knock at the door.

RAKER: Someone's here. Quick. *(Motions to kitchen hall.)*

ANYA *(not moving):* You'll be there?

RAKER: All right. I'll be there. *(Another knock.)* Now come along...you'll have to go out the back way.

As they exit, NATASHA *comes in to answer the knock. She is surprised to see her mother still there.*

NATASHA: Mother?

ANYA: Don't forget about Mr. Teesol.

NATASHA: Of course not.

RAKER: Mr. Teesol?

ANYA: Yes. Mr. Teesol.

RAKER: Come along, Mrs. Burke...this way.

NATASHA *lets in* SHRIKE *and* INK. SHRIKE *wears a morning suit and a top hat, kid leather gloves, and carries a walking cane.* INK *wears a rumpled business suit.*

SHRIKE: Tell the Mayor Mr. Shrike is here.

INK*(to* SHRIKE): And Mr. Ink.

NATASHA*(reluctantly):* Yes, sir. *(She goes off to the kitchen.)*

SHRIKE *deposits his cane in the stand.*

INK: Do you think he'll do it?

SHRIKE: That's what we're going to ask him.

Taking off the kid gloves, SHRIKE *holds them draped in one hand.*

INK: If this deal goes through –

SHRIKE: Yes, there's a fortune to be made...if you know the right people.

INK: And you know the right people, don't you Shrike?

SHRIKE: Yes, Ink, I do...I certainly do.

RAKER *enters.*

RAKER: Ah...Mr. Shrike. How's business with the CPR?

SHRIKE: It will be fine once we get rid of the Crow rates, and the branch lines and the passenger service.

INK: And stop being a railway?

SHRIKE: Of course not.

RAKER: You weren't at our last rehearsal for the operetta, Mr. Shrike.

SHRIKE: I had to spend some time in Moose...in Moose Jaw. After all, it is the Divisional Point.

RAKER: You didn't have to make it the Divisional Point.

SHRIKE: I didn't want to make it the divisional point. It was the Board of Directors in Montreal. They've never been to Moose...to Moose....

INK: To Moose Jaw.

SHRIKE: Yes. But we haven't come to talk about the CPR, Mr. Mayor.

RAKER: Of course not. What is it you have in mind?

SHRIKE: An opportunity, Mr. Mayor…an opportunity to make more than a little money.

RAKER: I'm listening.

INK: I've got some land!

SHRIKE: *We've* got some land. Mr. Ink purchased it from a farmer. One section at seven dollars an acre. He cleared the title through the Land Office yesterday.

RAKER: That's a good enough price.

INK: It's around the Wascana Marsh.

RAKER: I see. I didn't know you had taken a fancy to the farming life, Ink.

SHRIKE: We're not thinking of using it for farming.

INK: Go ahead, Shrike, tell him! Tell him!

SHRIKE: As you know, Mr. Mayor, every member of the Provincial Assembly is in town, to help give Saskatchewan its first anniversary present.

RAKER: Yes, to choose the new capital of the Province.

INK: Exactly!

SHRIKE: And I don't think it should be Moo…should be Moo….

INK: Moose Jaw.

SHRIKE: Yes. And as for Saskatoon –

INK: That teetotal town up north shouldn't stand a chance. Why, they didn't even have a bar until 1902.

SHRIKE: But Regina, now. Yes, Regina is prospering. The new City Hall is going up, thanks to you, Mr. Mayor.

INK: Yes, and a new Post Office!

SHRIKE: We're at the heart of the most fertile area in Canada!

RAKER*(they have struck a nerve):* It's true, it's true! We have ten thousand people here now! And our climate is unsurpassed anywhere – the weather is dry, clear and bright at least three hundred days of the year!

INK: But what about the winter?

SHRIKE *(a delicate whap with the gloves):* Ink.

RAKER: We're the wealthiest municipal corporation in the nation! We're paving South Railway! We're paving Scarth! We're paving all of Eleventh Avenue! No more will travellers from Toronto call us the mud-hole of the west. We're putting granolithic sidewalks everywhere!

INK *(dumbfounded):* Grano – what?

SHRIKE *(the gloves):* Cement, Ink, cement! Like your head.

RAKER: Our city is built in the middle of a vast plain, it has room to grow in all directions. It is neither confined by valleys nor divided by rivers. And yet gentlemen, and yet we have a practically inexhaustible supply of the purest water in Western Canada.

INK: Water, never touch the stuff.

SHRIKE *(the gloves):* Of course, Mr. Mayor, of course. And after Regina has been chosen the provincial capital....

RAKER: We'll need a site for the new Legislature.

INK *(astounded):* That's it!!

RAKER: Which, as you gentlemen already know, the Chief Returning Officer for the Province –

INK *(utterly astounded):* That's you!!

SHRIKE: Yes, Ink, yes.

RAKER: – which I will select.

SHRIKE: It could already be selected...in case of the vote actually turning out in favour of Regina.

RAKER: That's very true. However, I have already chosen a spot for the new Legislative Building.

INK *(downcast):* Oh no, we're too late.

RAKER *(walks to window overlooking park):* Yes. Standing here at my front window, looking out across this lovely park, I've often thought to myself....

SHRIKE: Yes?

INK: Yes?

SHRIKE: Yes?

RAKER: ...that if a small dam were built at the west end of Wascana Marsh it would create a beautiful lake. A perfect setting for a magnificent new Government Building.

INK *(astounded at this fortunate coincidence):* Then the spot you've already chosen is right in the middle of *our* land! *(Jumps in air.)* Whoopee!

SHRIKE: Yes, Ink, it is. And with the Government willing to pay at least three hundred dollars an acre –

INK: How did you know that?

SHRIKE *(losing patience):* I'm not the Party Whip for nothing!

INK: Party Whip? Which party?

SHRIKE: Which party is in power?

INK: Uh...the Liberals.

SHRIKE: Then I'm a Liberal.

INK: But I thought you were a Conservative?

RAKER: Last year he was. Come to think of it, so was I.

INK: Aha.

SHRIKE: But this year I'm a Liberal – and the Party Whip.

INK: I see – *(light dawning)* – ah, of course, I see. Three hundred dollars an acre. And I only paid seven. We'll be rich. *(Starts doing calculations in the air.)*

SHRIKE: Of course, the CPR want Moo...want Moo...want –

INK: Moose Jaw.

SHRIKE: To be the capital.

RAKER: That's perfectly understandable. They own every inch of it. But gentleman – *(Begins "We're the Ones." Sings.)*

We're the ones, yes, we're the very ones

SHRIKE & INK: We're the ones?

RAKER:

Who know which way the vote is going to go!
We're the ones, oh we're the very ones

SHRIKE & INK: We're the ones!

RAKER: Who know which way the wind is going to blow!

SHRIKE: We're the ones who're gonna make the dough

INK: The dough!

SHRIKE: Cause we know which way the gravy's gonna flow

RAKER:

Watch it flow!
It's such a pleasant feeling, don't you know

SHRIKE & INK: We know!

RAKER: To know how fast your money's gonna grow

INK: It's gonna grow!

ALL *(chorus):* We're all friends, yes we're all friends right here

RAKER: Of course we are!

They smile at each other, then RAKER *and* SHRIKE *pretend to stab* INK *in the back, as they sing.*

ALL: But who knows if we'll all be friends come around next year?

End chorus.

RAKER & SHRIKE: We're the ones, yes we're the very ones.

ALL:

Who know which way the vote is gonna go!
We're the ones, yes we're the very ones

INK: We're the ones!

ALL: Who know which way the wind is gonna blow!

Singing stops. Music continues under the following speeches.

RAKER: Now, gentlemen. We need a public transfer of the deed so that the land will be available for us to sell the moment Regina is chosen.

INK: A public transfer?! That's impossible! As soon as we let anyone know –

RAKER: It is required by the Land Act.

INK: It is?

SHRIKE *(sarcastic):* You are a lawyer, aren't you, Ink?

INK: Sure, but my secretary takes care of all the simple stuff.

SHRIKE: This would seem to be our final problem, Mr. Mayor.

INK: But we can't make a transfer of the deed openly!

RAKER: You do not believe in honesty in politics, Mr. Ink?

INK: I don't know about politics. But nobody ever got anywhere in the law by being honest.

SHRIKE: It is the perfect profession for you, then. Perhaps you can even become a judge.

INK: A judge? A judge! Of course! I'll be a judge!!

RAKER: Enough, my friends, enough. Let's not worry about the public transfer now. I'll think of something.

INK: I'm thinking about money! Beautiful money!

They all begin to sing again, with gusto.

SHRIKE: It gives us such a thrill and such a glow

INK: A glow!

SHRIKE: To know which way the gravy's gonna flow

INK: How it flows!

RAKER: We're on the top, we're so much in the know

ALL: Just look at how our money's gonna grow!

Music vamps and they do a dance like a minuet, then sing the chorus.

ALL: We're all friends, yes we're all friends right here

RAKER: Of course we are!

ALL:

But who knows if we'll all be friends come around next year?
(End chorus.)
We're the ones, yes we're the very ones

INK: We're the ones!

ALL:

Who know which way the vote is gonna go
We're the ones, oh we're the very ones

INK: We're the ones!

ALL: Just look at how our money's gonna grow

RAKER: And grow and grow

SHRIKE: And grow and grow

INK: And grow and grow!

SHRIKE: Gr-o-o-ow!!

RAKER: Gr-o-o-o-o-ow!!

INK *(off key):* Grow!!!

ALL: And grow and grow!

Song ends. ALICE *and* PERCY *enter.* ALICE *applauds.*

ALICE: Bravo Father! Bravo gentlemen! *(Laughs.)* You're going to be the hit of the operetta tonight!

INK *(astonished to see* PERCY, *the reporter):* Has he been here all the time?!

SHRIKE (the gloves)*:* Ink!

RAKER*:* We're not practising for the operetta...this is...is a meeting of City Council.

PERCY*:* Of course it is...and this is the usual song and dance.

ALICE *and* PERCY *laugh.*

ALICE: But Mr. Shrike and Mr. Ink aren't on City Council.

RAKER: I am the Mayor. And whenever I meet with anyone, it is just the same as if the entire Council has met with them.

ALICE: Oh, Father!

PERCY: Is there a story here for *The Leader*, Mr. Mayor?

RAKER: No story at all, Mr. Thistle.

INK *(nervous):* No, none at all, simply nothing, nobody would be interested, there's not a –

SHRIKE *(the gloves):* Ink!!

PERCY: Not even a rumour?

INK: Who started a rumour?

PERCY: About the choosing of the new capital perhaps?

RAKER *(jumps in):* Saskatoon has a strong claim. It has wonderfully wide streets.

INK: Dirt streets.

SHRIKE: Ink.

RAKER: Lots of pure river water.

INK: And a typhoid epidemic every year.

SHRIKE: Ink!

RAKER: And a population of over three thousand sober, industrious citizens.

INK: They're sober all right, too sober for a government town.

SHRIKE: Ink! Shut up! *(Gloves again.)*

INK: Oh...yes...Saskatoon would be the perfect place for the capital.

RAKER: Exactly what I was saying.

PERCY: Although, as Mayor, you will of course be doing your best for Regina.

RAKER: Of course. Just as you, being from Saskatoon, will do all you can for that city.

PERCY: Certainly. You've just admitted that Saskatoon has all the natural advantages. And that's precisely what I've said in this Special Issue of the paper.

RAKER: As long as you gave Regina its due as the economic heart of the province.

SHRIKE: And said Moo...said Moo....

INK: Moose Jaw.

SHRIKE: Is the transportation centre.

PERCY: My editor wouldn't want me to say anything less. *(Pause.)* But if you weren't talking about the choosing of the capital, what were you discussing, Mr. Mayor?

RAKER *(cool):* The Wascana Marsh, Mr. Thistle. The Wascana Marsh.

INK *(terrified):* The Wascana –

PERCY: It's a stinking swamp.

RAKER: It's a practically inexhaustible supply of the purest water in Western Canada!

PERCY *(laughs):* I did an analysis of that liquid. And there were beetles, two parts, tadpoles, five. Not dead, oh no, all very much alive. Pure mud I placed at seventy, and the rest – all twenty-three per cent – was some kind of murky fluid. I'll call it "water," if you like that name the best!

ALICE *laughs.*

RAKER: The City administration is doing the best it can for Regina.

SHRIKE: Of course it is. And so is the CPR.

PERCY: Is that why you moved your Divisional Point to Moose Jaw?

PERCY *and* ALICE *laugh.* INK *joins in, then is stopped dead by a scorching look from* SHRIKE.

SHRIKE *(exploding):* Criticize the CPR would you?! People do not give the CPR enough credit for what it has done for this country! Look at our beautiful stations, our splendid hotels, our nine thousand miles of gleaming track. The track...oh, it's incredible track...eighty pound rails of steel made to our detailed specifications...resting upon solid wooden ties, thirty million of them...do you know that's ten train loads of ties a week!? A week!? Credit? Oh no, we don't get any credit! We get accusations! Accusations!! The CPR was given twenty-five million dollars and twenty-five million acres of crown land to build the railroad ...that's what they say. What if we were?! That land only became worth anything because we built the railroad through it. Yes! It was the main line of the CPR that made this feeble, knock-kneed whelp of a country into a nation!

SHRIKE *has moved to* PERCY *and* ALICE, *and at last snaps out of it, bowing low before her.*

Ah, Miss Raker. It is such a great pleasure to see you again. *(Quickly takes her hand and kisses it.)*

ALICE *(startled):* Aaaahh!

SHRIKE*:* You are looking so very elegant today. You bring such a grace to this wild country. You are like a goddess of civilization.

ALICE*:* Percy!

PERCY*:* Yes?

INK*:* She is awfully pretty.

SHRIKE *(ignores* PERCY*):* Pretty?! Pretty is far too common a word for Miss Raker. She is everything a young lady should be. Perhaps, Mr. Mayor, you and your daughter would like to join me for the opening of our new hotel in Winnipeg later this month...the Royal Alexandra. We could go in my special coach.

ALICE: Percy, we were going to plan a picnic in Lumsden.

PERCY: We were?

SHRIKE: Miss Raker, would you and your father care to join me for lunch at the Assiniboia Club?

ALICE: I'm sorry, but I'm already engaged for lunch. Aren't I, Percy?

PERCY: Oh...yes. Alice and I are having lunch together.

SHRIKE: I see, I see. And I suppose you have that immigration pamphlet all ready for me.

PERCY: Which immigration pamphlet? I'm working on a dozen or more.

SHRIKE: The one about women. You know. The need for cultivated women on the prairies.

PERCY: Oh, that one. Sure, I've got it right here. It's almost done.

SHRIKE: Well, I need it right away!

RAKER: Mr. Shrike...Mr. Shrike. Don't you remember we still have a few details to work out in regard to...to the City of Regina dinner this evening?

SHRIKE: Ah...yes...a few details. Of course. Miss Raker. *(Bows and tries to kiss her hand again. She will not let him.)* I may have the pleasure of your company another time then.

INK: The dinner? But what about the...you know?

RAKER: You're right. I did promise you a drink, didn't I?

INK: A drink?

RAKER: Yes, a drink. Come along, Mr. Ink. We'll have a drink...a drink to a fortunate future.

INK: It's never too early to break out the booze!

RAKER: And we'll take our politics to the back room – where they belong. *(Beckons.)* Mr. Shrike.

They exit, singing and doing a minuet chorus line.

RAKER, INK & SHRIKE:

We're the ones, yes we're the very ones!
We're the ones, yes we're the very ones!
We're the ones, yes we're the very ones!

PERCY *looks after them with curiosity.*

PERCY: I'm beginning to think....

ALICE: Percy....

PERCY: ...there's something....

ALICE: I've been thinking.

PERCY: Something going on. The Mayor....

ALICE: Percy?

PERCY: ...a lawyer and the Liberal Party Whip....

ALICE: That's who I'm taking about.

PERCY: Who?

ALICE: Mr. Shrike. Now look, Percy, things are getting pretty serious.

PERCY: Yes, they certainly are.

ALICE: I mean, with Mr. Shrike.

PERCY: Yes, I know.

ALICE: And there's our feelings.

PERCY: Yes....

ALICE: Your feelings and my feelings.

PERCY: You have this feeling too?

ALICE: We're going to have to do something soon!

PERCY: I know, I know.

ALICE: Or that Mr. Shrike –

PERCY: Shrike! Yes. That's what I can't –

ALICE: Isn't it obvious?!

PERCY: Exactly! It should be obvious!

ALICE: Percy!!

PERCY: Yes?

ALICE: Percy, listen to me. It's a beautiful day. It's summer. We should really go for a ride out to the valley. The saskatoon berries are all ripe!

PERCY: I'm sorry. I don't have that CPR pamphlet ready for Mr. Shrike, and then I have to work on…on something else!

ALICE: But what about our picnic?

PERCY: We can go to the valley tomorrow.

ALICE: At least let's go for a walk over to the marsh before you have to work.

PERCY: Well, okay….

ALICE: Good. I'll tell Father where we're going.

ALICE *goes off to the back room.* NATASHA *enters. She has been waiting for him to be alone.*

NATASHA: Mr. Thistle?

PERCY *(stunned):* What?! Oh. Yes, Natasha?

NATASHA: I wonder if I could ask you something.

PERCY: Sure.

NATASHA: I mean, it's a favour.

PERCY: Well, after a breakfast like that, how can I refuse you anything?

NATASHA: Would you be able to write a report on a meeting my mother has helped organize?

PERCY: A Dominion Day tea and bake sale? Of course.

NATASHA: It's not exactly that.

PERCY: No?

NATASHA: No. It's a meeting to support the cause of Women's Suffrage.

PERCY: Ah. I see. A radical meeting.

NATASHA: I don't see it that way.

PERCY: Of course not. Your mother helped organize it.

NATASHA: Well, will you do it? Please.

PERCY: When does it start?

NATASHA: It's in the park at noon. *(Excited.)* There's a speaker all the way from Winnipeg, and –

PERCY: Now, now…I'm sure it's nothing to get excited about. But I'll be there. *(Pause.)* As a favour to you.

NATASHA: Thank you, Mr. Thistle.

PERCY: I've told you to call me Percy. Say, I'm still a bit hungry. Do you think I could have a piece of your special saskatoon pie?

NATASHA: Of course. I'll get one for you.

PERCY: Oh, don't bother. I may want more than one. *(He offers his arm.)* Let me escort you back to the kitchen.

NATASHA: Oh…all right. *(Takes his arm.)* And thank you very much for agreeing –

PERCY: Don't worry about that. The least I can do is treat this meeting of yours as an entertainment and do a review! *(He laughs.)*

NATASHA: It's a serious meeting, Mr. Thistle.

PERCY: Percy's the name. Percy.

They exit. ALICE *and her father come on. He looks for and gets another bottle from the sideboard.*

ALICE: …so Percy and I are going for a walk in the park.

RAKER: Don't go there. *(Looks in sideboard.)*

ALICE: Why not?

RAKER: There's going to be a meeting.

ALICE: What kind of meeting?

RAKER *(gets bottle):* Nothing you'd be interested in. Only a bunch of women who don't know how to act like ladies.

ALICE *(somewhat interested):* Oh...the Suffrage crowd.

RAKER: I understand they're bringing in some rabble-rouser. I'm going along just to keep an eye on things.

ALICE: When is it?

RAKER: Noon.

ALICE: We'll just go for a short stroll then, and I'll bring Percy back here for lunch.

RAKER: Not just the two of you?

ALICE: I think Percy's pretty serious about me.

RAKER: If you could judge that by the number of meals he has around here, I'd have to agree.

ALICE: I think he might even ask me to marry him.

RAKER: I wouldn't doubt it.

ALICE: Then you approve!

RAKER: I didn't say that. He's only a penniless junior reporter.

ALICE: He won't be for long.

RAKER: No, he might not even be that if he starts poking his nose in where it doesn't belong.

ALICE: Please, Father.

RAKER: You know, Mr. Shrike has a very good position with the CPR. And I think he's about to come into quite a lot of money.

ALICE: Mr. Shrike! But I love Percy.

RAKER: The answer is no!

ALICE: But Father –

INK & SHRIKE *(off, singing):* We're the ones, yes we're the very ones! *(Laughter)*

RAKER: I've got to get back to my meeting.

He leaves. INK *cheers as he sees the new bottle.*

INK *(off):* Hurrah! More booze!

ALICE: But Father...*(parodies* SHRIKE) "Miss Raker, you are looking so very elegant today. You bring such a grace to this wild country." *(Looks at hand he kissed.)* Uughh! *(Wipes it on her dress. Calls out.)* Percy? Percy, where are you?

PERCY *appears from the kitchen, finishing the last forkful of a piece of saskatoon pie.* NATASHA *follows. He hands her the plate and fork.*

ALICE: Thank you, Natasha, that's all. *(Takes* PERCY*'s arm.)* Let's go to the park now, Percy.

PERCY *(wipes lips with handkerchief):* Sure. We can see if they've planted any new trees higher than...*(Puts hands on her hips.)*...higher than your waist!

They laugh and go off, out the front door. NATASHA, *holding the plate and fork, looks longingly after* PERCY. *Music begins for "Saskatoon Pie."*

NATASHA (sings):

Wouldn't you like to pick berries with me
In the warm sunshine, down in the ravine
Baskets of saskatoons, purple and sweet
And we'll make pie out of what we don't eat

Oh, oh, saskatoon pie!
I'll give you a piece of my saskatoon pie!

All of the bushes are heavy and sway
With berries ripe in the heat of the day
They'll fall in our hands and burst on our tongues
Filling our mouths full of juice from the sun

Oh, oh, saskatoon pie!
We'll share a piece of sweet saskatoon pie!

Or down on the bank of the creek we could lie
Through dancing leaves watch clouds drifting by
Ripples of water will carry our dreams
Into a future that flows like the stream

Oh, oh, saskatoon pie!
Oh-oh-oh-oh, saskatoon pie!
Oh-oh-oh-oh, saskatoon pie!
Can't you just taste that sweet saskatoon pie?
Can't you just taste that sweet saskatoon pie?

Blackout.

SCENE TWO

ANYA*'s house. Enter* JEAN *and* ANYA. JEAN *carries a poster brush and a pot of glue.*

ANYA: Well, there's the posters done.

JEAN: Och aye! There isn't a naked telephone pole in the entire city! They're all decently covered now!

ANYA: We'll have to keep our voices down. She's sleeping in the back bedroom.

JEAN: Ahh…recovering from the effects of a night ride in a CPR day coach.

ANYA: Yes, she is.

JEAN: The CPR made that train arrive at 3:33 A.M. just to spite Regina because it was made capital of the Northwest Territories instead of Moose Jaw. That was in 1882, and if Regina is now chosen capital of the new province of Saskatchewan, I'm afraid that train will be arriving at 3:33 A.M. until 2082! Of course, my hopes are pinned on Saskatoon. The fortress of Temperance! *(Back to guest.)* What's she like?

ANYA *(hesitant):* Well...she was so tired it was hard to tell anything really.

JEAN: What's the trouble?

ANYA: She seemed somewhat...somewhat shy.

JEAN: Shy?! That's all we need in our featured speaker.

ANYA: We must give her a chance, Jean.

JEAN: One chance is all she'll have at the meeting. And if she can't make the most of it...what's her name?

ANYA: Her name?

JEAN: Aye. What's the lassie's name?

ANYA: I think it's...*(Trouble saying it.)*...La-tee-sja.

JEAN: That's Letitia.

ANYA: Le-tee-sha?

JEAN: Letitia is a very fine Scottish name. Unfortunately, there's no punch to it. No fire!!

ANYA: I think she has another name.

JEAN: Thank goodness for small mercies.

ANYA: There were two initials on her travelling bag, as well as her last name. But her name doesn't matter, as long as she can give a speech.

JEAN: Aye. We were promised a strong speaker. Someone to make the men tremble in their boots. The Mayor will be coming to the meeting?

ANYA: I'm sure he'll be there. With all his friends, including your boss, Mr. Ink.

JEAN: That fool! He doesn't know a writ from a tort! Or a tort from a pie! Even when he's sober. But I think he's up to something...I always prepare the documents, but only yesterday he sent me away from the typewriter and tried to do some himself. It's pitiful to see his poor stupefied brain trying to separate a caveat from a codicil. *(Shouts.)* The man's an idiot!

ANYA: Jean, shh, shh.

LETITIA *enters, rubbing the sleep from her eyes.*

LETITIA: Excuse me.

ANYA: Oh, my goodness.

JEAN: I'm sorry, lassie. I forgot you were resting.

LETITIA: Oh, that's all right. Please don't worry. I do have to do a bit more work on my speech. I had rather short notice about Mrs. Hjartasson not being able to come.

JEAN: You mean, you're a substitute?!

ANYA: If Mrs...*(Trouble with name.)* Huh-har – if the Manitoba Suffrage League sent you, you must be very good indeed.

JEAN: Mrs. Hjartasson?

LETITIA: She's president of the League. And Hjartasson is a very fine Icelandic name.

JEAN: Och aye.

LETITIA: And she's sorry she can't be here, but she sends her regards to all of you who are engaged in the struggle for Votes for Women in Saskatchewan.

ANYA: That is very nice of her.

LETITIA *(trying out a phrase from her speech):* It's women like Mrs. Hjartasson who laid the foundation upon which we are going to build the house of women's rights.

JEAN: A solid foundation is what we need to stand on when we're swinging the hammer of truth! *(Changing subject.)* Now, what about that speech? It isn't finished, you said?

ANYA *(cutting this off):* Letitia will have plenty of time for that, as long as we give her breakfast first.

JEAN: I can give you a hand if you run into any difficulty in what to say. It's just a good thing we don't have any more rehearsals for the operetta.

LETITIA: An operetta? What operetta?

JEAN: It's called *Magic Reversals*. *Magic Reversals*, ha!

ANYA: Women are given power.

JEAN: For one night.

ANYA: Yes, and they don't know what to do, but they try to stay in charge.

JEAN: And dreadful disasters happen, and the men have to seize control again. Of course. How else could it possibly turn out?

LETITIA: Then why are you in it?

JEAN: My boss, Mr. Ink, told me I had to be in it or I'd lose my job. Ha! Without me to instruct him in the proper use of the law, that drunkard would be bankrupt in a wink!

LETITIA: They aren't worried about you organizing this meeting?

JEAN: Oh, they think that's another joke.

ANYA: They are not yet worried enough about our work for the Vote to do anything. We hope they will start more when they hear you speak.

JEAN: Aye, we *hope* they will. A substitute, you say?

ANYA: Now, Jean. If you'd like to get dressed, Letitia, I'll fix you something to eat. You must be hungry.

LETITIA: Yes, I am, a little.

ANYA: We'll have a nice big breakfast.

JEAN: Aye. You're going to need something that'll stick to your stomach when you meet the Mayor and his cronies.

ANYA: The newspaper should be there too. My daughter, Natasha, is going to invite that young reporter, Mr. Teesol.

JEAN: That's Thistle, lassie, Thistle. Scotland's national emblem. It's a beautiful flower defended by thorns – and there's a lesson there for all women to learn.

ANYA: Well, the reporter should be there too.

JEAN: Although that might not do us any good. He's strong for temperance, but he was not sympathetic when I spoke to him about the need for women to have the Vote. He asked me what possible interest women could have in politics? What interest in politics, when Demon Drink rules the land, ruining the lives of poor women and wee innocent babes?!

She launches into "Demon Drink," unnerving LETITIA. ANYA *echoes the words.*

JEAN *(sings):* Oh Demon Drink!

ANYA *(sings):* Oh Demon Drink!

JEAN:

It's far worse than you think
It takes a man to the brink
And shoves him over!
Oh Demon Drink!

ANYA: Oh Demon Drink!

JEAN:

It's far worse than you think
It takes a man to the brink
And shoves him down!

JEAN & ANYA:

Oh we have tried to get all men to take the pledge
To never, ever touch a drop of Demon Drink again
And only if the cause of Temperance could prevail
This world would be a better place – Amen!

JEAN: Oh in saloons

ANYA: Oh in saloons

JEAN:

Where old Alcohol is King
Whatever life you bring him

He destroys it!
But when he hears

ANYA: But when he hears

JEAN:

Our Union marching near
Why then he trembles in his fear
And runs away!

Having got over her initial shock, LETITIA joins in.

CHORUS:
Oh we have tried to get all men to take the pledge
To never, ever touch a drop of Demon Drink again
And only if the cause of Temperance could prevail
This world would be a better place – Amen!

JEAN: The Liquor Trade

ANYA & LETITIA: The Liquor Trade

JEAN:

Needs young men to be its slaves
And wherever it can catch them
It exploits them!
It lures them on

ANYA & LETITIA: It lures them on

JEAN:

Six thousand every year
And their sweethearts, wives and children
Rue the day!

ANYA & LETITIA: They rue that day!

ALL:

That Demon Drink (oh Demon Drink)
It's far worse than you think
It takes a man to the brink
And shoves him over!
Oh Demon Drink (oh Demon Drink)

It's far worse than you think
It takes a man to the brink
And throws him down!
It throws him down!!
It takes a man to the brink
And throws him down!
It throws him down!!
It takes a man to the brink
And throws him down!!!

Song ends.

JEAN: Now, about that speech.

ANYA: Breakfast first, Jean. If you'd like to get dressed, Letitia.

LETITIA: Yes, I will.

ANYA: We'll get breakfast ready.

LETITIA: Thank you.

Music vamp begins again.

JEAN: She seems a bit of a green girl.

ANYA: I'm sure the Manitoba women know what they're doing. She'll be fine.

JEAN: Well, she doesn't seem fierce enough to me.

ANYA: Things said quietly may also have their effect, Jean.

JEAN *(shouts):* But once ye're in the thick of the fray, ye have to be heerd!!

ANYA: Let's stoke the fires then.

JEAN: Aye! And prepare for battle!

LETITIA *amazingly emerges, fully dressed.*

LETITIA *(sings):*

We are marching on in the fight
In the fight

JEAN & ANYA *(sing):* In the fight

LETITIA: For womens' rights!

JEAN & ANYA: For womens' rights!

LETITIA:

We are marching on in the fight
Organizing with all our might!

ALL:

Oh we must try to get women all to take a pledge
To never, ever have the Vote belong only to men
For if only the cause of Suffrage could prevail
This world would be a better place – Amen!

Blackout.

Scene Three

Outdoors. A beautiful prairie day in the park near the Wascana Marsh. The PIANO PLAYER *plays a bird whistle.* PERCY *and* ALICE *stroll on arm in arm. There is a park bench.*

ALICE: It's such a gorgeous day!

PERCY: Enjoy it while you can...it's Saskatchewan's version of summer.

ALICE: Oh, Percy, really.

PERCY: Too late for mosquitoes. *(He whaps his arm.)* Almost. Too early for a blizzard. We hope. It's the only place in the entire world where you can wake up one morning and say, "Summer's here!" and wake up the next morning and say, "Well, that was nice!"

ALICE: But feel how wonderful that sun is now. It's so warm. Percy?

PERCY: Yes?

ALICE: Wouldn't you like to go someplace where it's always warm?

PERCY: Like Saskatoon?

ALICE: No, like British Columbia. I hear it's always summer in British Columbia.

PERCY: It must be awfully dull in British Columbia. The weather here is so dramatic!

ALICE: The mountains are dramatic – and there are lots of mountains in British Columbia.

PERCY: I like my landscape flat. It's easier to walk on.

ALICE *(a bit scornful):* And wonderful for farming.

PERCY: Which is exactly what I say in my pamphlet for Mr. Shrike and the CPR. *(Pulls out paper.)*

ALICE: So you've nearly got it finished?

PERCY: Just a few more touches.

ALICE: Then maybe we can still go pick berries this afternoon.

PERCY: Maybe. But listen, what do you think of this? *(Reads.)* "There is no life more idyllic and healthy for women than life on a farm in Saskatchewan. There, women who prefer a temperate and rational existence may prosper."

ALICE: It sounds wonderful. But Percy....

PERCY: There's more. "They should be women of culture, who have had training in the domestic arts by practising them, but who will keep up the tone of the men with whom they mix by music and book lore when the day's work is done."

ALICE: Percy, haven't you left something out?

PERCY: No, I'm not finished. "The same pair of hands, busy with a butter-pat in the morning may in the afternoon guide the embroidery needle, or with the palette reproduce a bit of local colour." There. That's it. Now what have I left out?

ALICE: Oh, cows and chickens and pigs and weeding the garden and baking bread and prairie fires and have you ever lived on a farm?

PERCY: Lived on a farm? No. I grew up on Temperance Street, and I've never even been on a farm. But neither have most of the people who'll read this.

ALICE: Well, it doesn't seem quite honest…telling fibs for the CPR.

PERCY: How else are you gonna get people to come out here? Do you think they'd homestead if I told them the truth about blizzards and forty below?!

ALICE: Which is precisely why I mentioned British Columbia. Look, Percy, wouldn't you like to have your own paper? Percy Thistle, Editor. Don't you like the sound of it?

PERCY: Sure, but I don't make a lot even working for *The Leader* and doing stuff for the CPR too. Certainly not enough to start my own paper.

ALICE: Well, Percy, if we're serious about each other –

PERCY: Well, sure.

ALICE: Then you better start thinking about British Columbia and getting me away from Mr. Shrike.

PERCY: Mr. Shrike!

ALICE: My father wants me to marry Mr. Shrike. And he also told me that Mr. Shrike is about to come into quite a lot of money.

PERCY: His share of another CPR land deal, I bet.

ALICE: Percy, I'm worried.

PERCY *(arm around her, playful):* Aww, don't you worry about him. *(Jumps up on bench, sniffs.)* Phew! There's the marsh. *(He helps her get up beside him.)*

ALICE: It smells so…so earthy!

PERCY: "Earthy?" That isn't quite the word I'd use. But say…*(Looks out over marsh, that is, the audience)* if they put a dam over there, to the west, see, it'd back up the water. That'd kill the smell.

ALICE: Then what?

PERCY: Then you'd have a lake…well, maybe not a real lake, but enough of a lake that you – *(Stops with a sudden idea. Jumps into air from bench.)* That's it! *(Lands.)* That's what they're all up to! What a story!

ALICE: Percy!

PERCY: Don't worry about Shrike. I'll take care of him.

ALICE: You will?

PERCY: Yes. But I have to see...see...someone about...something ...about something very important right away.

ALICE: I was going to ask you home to lunch.

PERCY: Home? No. Home. Don't go there.

ALICE: I could get Natasha to fix you something special.

PERCY: No. Don't do that. I'll tell you what. Yes. You wait for me here. I won't be long, and then I'll come back and meet you...*(He starts to leave.)*

ALICE: But there's going to be a meeting.

PERCY *(returning):* Oh. The meeting. Well, I said I'd do a story on the meeting.

ALICE: My father won't like it.

PERCY: How will he know until he's seen it?

ALICE: Of course he'll see it, he's going to be at the meeting.

PERCY: No, the story.

ALICE: No. Not the story. I mean he won't like my being at the meeting.

PERCY: Oh, the meeting!

ALICE: It's a Suffrage meeting. They want the Vote.

PERCY: You don't want the Vote, do you? Not when you've got me. I can vote for both of us.

ALICE: Oh, Percy, do you mean that?

PERCY: Well, *you* can't vote, can you?

ALICE: No. I mean that I've got you. That you love me.

PERCY: Oh, that. Sure I love you. But look, it won't matter if you stay.

ALICE: Stay here?

PERCY: Sure. *(He starts to leave.)*

ALICE: But my father –

PERCY *(returns):* He won't make any fuss about it. Trust me.

ALICE: I do trust you. I'll wait...I'll wait as long as you want.

PERCY: Good. I'll be back in time for the meeting. It'll be around here someplace. *(He starts to leave again.)*

ALICE *(calls):* Percy!

PERCY *(pauses):* Yes?

ALICE: Don't forget we have to practice our duet for the operetta.

PERCY: Okay. Later.

ALICE: And Percy!

PERCY: Yes?

ALICE: I love you! *(She wafts a kiss his way.)*

PERCY: Sure. *(He runs off.)*

ALICE *gets down from the bench and sings "Hot Prairie Sun."*

ALICE:

Oh how that hot prairie sun
Fills up the sky with its light
And oh how my love fills my heart
Making it shine through the night

Now I have found you
I have to be round you
Never too far from your arms
You hold me so warmly
I'll never be lonely
We'll always keep our love safe from all harm

You breathe, you be
You are more than I ever dreamed

As ALICE *sings, lights go down on the rest of the park, isolating her. If possible, staging should be arranged so that lights can also come up in the Mayor's house. Possibly the "park" is at the front of the stage with a scrim behind. Then* NATASHA, *in the Mayor's house, can also be spotlighted as she joins in on the final verse and chorus.* ALICE *and* NATASHA *sing together, although they are in different places.*

ALICE & NATASHA:

Oh how that hot prairie sun
Fills up the sky with its light
And oh how my love shines on me
Warming me all through the night

When you have gone
It's so hard to go on
Without your smile or your touch
And when I kiss you
I can't resist you
I never knew I could love you so much

You breathe, you be
You breathe, you be
You are more than I ever dreamed

At the end of the song, ALICE *goes off, the scrim is removed and lights go up full on* NATASHA *and the Mayor's house.*

Scene Four

The Mayor's house. NATASHA, *carrying an empty picnic basket, is about to leave. She is just putting on her shawl, when, without knocking,* PERCY *bursts through the front door, almost knocking her over.*

NATASHA: Ohh!

PERCY: Natasha! I've figured it out! *(Grabs her arms.)*

NATASHA *(hoping, for one wild moment, he might have figured out her love for him):* You have?!

PERCY: Yes!

NATASHA: Oh, Percy!

PERCY: Are they still here?

NATASHA: Still here? Who?

PERCY: The Mayor, Shrike, Ink?

NATASHA: Yes.

PERCY: They haven't left?

NATASHA: What have you figured out?

PERCY: In the back room?

NATASHA: Yes.

PERCY: Wonderful!

PERCY *gives her a kiss. She is astonished, but likes it.* RAKER *enters, to get another bottle, while they are kissing.*

NATASHA: Yes, it is.

RAKER: What's going on here?

NATASHA: Oh! Nothing, sir.

PERCY *(cheeky):* It's a little secret between us, isn't it Natasha?

NATASHA *(does he love her??):* Our secret?

RAKER: Your secret, is it? *(To* NATASHA.) Is it any secret where you're off to now?

NATASHA: I have to do some shopping for lunch.

RAKER: Well, be on your way then. And fill that basket up. We'll be hungry.

NATASHA: Of course, sir. *(She puts on her shawl and exits, giving* PERCY *a longing look as she does.)*

RAKER: I thought you had gone for a walk with my daughter?

PERCY: I had...until I found out your secret.

RAKER: My secret? I thought it was your secret?

PERCY: No. It was your secret, but it's our secret now.

RAKER: You found this out from my daughter?

PERCY: From Alice?

RAKER *(annoyed):* Yes, what other daughter do I have? *(Quite worried, maybe* PERCY *does know about the other daughter.)* What kind of secret?

PERCY: It's not one you'd like everyone to know.

RAKER: But you told Natasha?

PERCY *(expansive):* Where are your partners?

RAKER: My partners? What do you mean?

PERCY *(calls out):* Mr. Ink! Mr. Shrike!

RAKER: What does this have to do with them?

PERCY: It has everything to do with them.

SHRIKE *and* INK *enter, drinking.* INK *is somewhat – although not completely – plastered. He carries the half-full bottle.*

SHRIKE: What's *he* doing here again?

PERCY: Gentlemen!

INK: Oh, it's Percy Whistle. Hello, Percy.

PERCY: Gentlemen, you are having a successful meeting?

INK: The gravy's gonna flow!

PERCY: Of course it is.

SHRIKE: You would be out of your depth in a mud puddle, Ink.

RAKER: Get to the point, Mr. Thistle.

PERCY: I have discovered a secret.

SHRIKE: What kind of secret?

PERCY: Your secret.

RAKER: *His* secret? I thought it was my secret?

INK: I've got a secret too!

PERCY: It is your secret as well, Mr. Ink.

RAKER: First it's your secret, then it's my secret, and now it's their secret! What secret?!

PERCY: It's a secret about the new....

INK: About the new....

PERCY *(pops it on* INK*):* About the new Legislature!

RAKER *(aside):* Ah...only that.

INK*:* But nobody knows about –

SHRIKE *(a smack with the gloves):* Ink!!

PERCY*:* That's why it's a secret!

INK *(relieved):* Of course. *(Laughs.)*

RAKER*:* What about the new Legislature, Mr. Thistle?

PERCY*:* The site, Mr. Mayor, the site.

SHRIKE*:* No one even knows what city will be chosen capital.

PERCY*:* The Premier is very confident. He has ordered a costly new printing press.

RAKER*:* Business is good these days. The city is growing by leaps and bounds.

PERCY*:* But if the Government moves out of Regina, it won't be much good at all.

INK*:* He's right there.

PERCY*:* But if it stays, business will certainly be better...especially for those who own land around Wascana Marsh.

INK*:* You said nobody knew!

SHRIKE *(a harder smack):* Whoever that may be.

PERCY*:* A title search would not be difficult to do.

RAKER*:* For an enterprising young reporter who hopes to make a name.

PERCY*:* Perhaps.

INK*:* His name could be mud.

SHRIKE*:* Ink.

RAKER*:* In any event, Mr. Thistle, it's a holiday…the Land Titles Office is closed, and by tomorrow….

PERCY*:* Every good journalist has contacts.

INK*:* The unspeakable arrogance of youth.

RAKER*:* Is one of its greatest charms, Mr. Ink. Well, Mr. Thistle, what do you propose?

PERCY*:* Propose? Oh yes, propose. Your daughter –

SHRIKE *(smiling):* Mr. Thistle.

PERCY*:* Mr. Shrike?

SHRIKE*:* I've been giving it a great deal of thought, and I don't think I'm paying you well enough for the work you've been doing for me.

PERCY *(surprised):* You're not?

SHRIKE*:* I think, if I paid you properly, you might be able to leave town and set up your own newspaper somewhere else…somewhere far away.

PERCY*:* Oh?

SHRIKE*:* Somewhere alone.

PERCY*:* Alone?

SHRIKE*:* I think you understand me, Mr. Thistle. How much does it cost to set up a paper? Say fifteen thousand dollars?

INK*:* Oh, it costs a lot more than that!

SHRIKE*:* Ink.

INK*:* I'd say at least four times that much!

SHRIKE *(the gloves):* Ink!

PERCY*:* He's right. Setting up a paper is getting more expensive all the time. *(To* INK.) You suggested sixty thousand dollars?

INK *(to* SHRIKE*):* That's nearly all you'd make on our deal.

SHRIKE *(fiercely):* Shut up, Ink.

INK: And if you didn't have that money, then you'd have to keep going to Moose Jaw.

SHRIKE: To Moo…to Moo…to Moo….

PERCY: Why do you have trouble saying that name?

SHRIKE: I don't have any trouble saying Moo…saying Moo…I don't have any trouble saying it at all. What I have trouble with is imagining a lifetime spent in visiting Moo…in visiting places like that! The CPR is doing its best to bring some measure of civilization to the west, but there is not much that even the CPR can do with a place like Moo…like Moo…

INK: I thought you liked riding back and forth to Moose Jaw on the train?

SHRIKE: The train? The train?! Of course I like riding on the train! The CPR has the most magnificent trains in the world! I love riding on the train! I have my own special coach with my own special seat all covered in blue velvet, and my own special rugs – soft, deep rugs laid over a floor of polished mahogany. And the walls, the walls are Circassian walnut with beautiful inlays of jacaranda, sycamore, chestnut, acacia, and teak…teak I tell you! The train! I love riding on the train! The vibration! Aaahhhhhhh! The perpetual trembling dance of body and marvellous machine thundering down the track, the endless track!! Faster and faster! *(Whistle noise.)* Whooo-whooo! Whooo-whooo! If only it never stopped! Never stopped! *(Like the wheels clicking.)* Never stopped! Never stopped! Never!! Especially at places like Moo…like Moo…like Mooo…like…I can't give up the money…Mr. Mayor! He can have her!! He can have Alice!!

RAKER: I see.

INK: Now why don't you leave, Mr. Whistle?

SHRIKE *(quieter):* Whooo-whooo!

PERCY: Gentlemen...I don't think we fully understand each other. You see, the other newspaper has approached me many times to work for them.

INK: The *West?!* That Conservative rag!

RAKER: But you have always refused them....

PERCY: Until now. But as you know, they are chomping at the bit for a nice juicy scandal that could bring the Government down.

RAKER *bursts out laughing.*

INK *(to* SHRIKE): What's he laughing for?

RAKER: I thought my daughter had her heart set on a fool, truly I did!

SHRIKE: How wrong you were...he isn't a fool at all.

RAKER *stops laughing abruptly.*

RAKER: What are your terms? Ten per cent after costs?

INK: You can give him your daughter, Mr. Mayor, but he's not getting any of my share of the money.

SHRIKE: One hundred per cent of nothing is nothing, Ink.

INK: It is?

RAKER: Well, I guess we better settle this now. There's the wedding, the honeymoon, and your new paper. Let's see....

PERCY *(to* INK): You said sixty thousand dollars was one share?

INK: It's actually ah....*(Tries to figure it out in the air. He can't do it.)*

RAKER *(going on):* It was – when there were three of us. Now there are four. So let's be joint partners...quarter shares. Agreed, Shrike?

PERCY: So a quarter share would be....

RAKER: Nearly fifty thousand dollars.

INK *(to* SHRIKE): But what if we can't arrange a public transfer of the deed?

SHRIKE *(several whaps with the gloves):* Will you never learn to keep your mouth shut?!

PERCY: That's right. How are you going to make the transfer public and keep it secret at the same time?

RAKER: Don't worry, I'm thinking about it. It's quite secure in my hands, Mr. Thistle.

PERCY *(thinking about the sum):* Fifty thousand dollars.

INK: And not a penny more!

SHRIKE: Come along, what more could you want?

PERCY *(not sure he should get into this):* I don't know....

RAKER: You've done very well for yourself, young fellow.

INK *(falls to knees):* C'mon Thistle. Make a deal. Please.

SHRIKE: We're waiting Mr. Thistle.

PERCY: Well...*(Deciding.)* All right. *(Puts out hand.)*

> RAKER, SHRIKE *&* INK *are seized with a fit of laughter.* INK *points at* PERCY*'s hand.*

SHRIKE: Shake hands with the devil, would you?

INK: We never shake hands on a deal, never!

RAKER: I forgot. You've led a sheltered life in Saskatoon.

PERCY: I learned a lot working for the paper there.

INK *(laughs):* He worked for the paper. He worked for *The Phoenix! (Laughs.)*

SHRIKE: It's a great paper if you've got a puppy! *(Laughs.)*

PERCY: It's a great paper even if you don't! *(Remembers his old allegiance.)* Saskatoon...if Saskatoon isn't made the capital and they hear I made a bundle from Regina getting it –

RAKER: Don't worry, Mr. Thistle. That will be *our* little secret. Anyway, we'll make sure Saskatoon gets that traffic bridge they've always wanted.

SHRIKE *(laughing):* The CPR has one we couldn't use in Winnipeg. It's too narrow. We'll give them that!

RAKER *(laughing):* And why not throw in a new station?

SHRIKE *(laughing):* All right. A new station. And a railway bridge.

RAKER *(laughing):* And a new Court House. We'll give them the one from Prince Albert.

INK *(having fits)*: And give them...give them the University!

RAKER: So you see, Mr. Thistle, Saskatoon will get what it deserves. Now, we always close our deals with a drink.

PERCY: I don't drink.

INK *(laughs):* He doesn't drink!

SHRIKE *(laughs):* Of course he doesn't drink! He's from Saskatoon!

INK *and* SHRIKE *both laugh.*

RAKER: What you mean is, you didn't drink. You're not an innocent young reporter any more. You're in politics now!

INK *takes a final swig of the bottle he's been carrying and hands it to* PERCY.

INK: Here. Go on, it won't bite.

RAKER: Bottoms up.

PERCY *takes a deep breath, tips the bottle up, and drinks it down, while the others sing.*

RAKER, SHRIKE & INK:

Booze, liquor, alcohol
Call it what you will
Hoist your glass, down the hatch!
Come on drink your fill!

Stingo, bung juice
Helps you feel no pain
Drive another nail boys!
Strip me naked once again!

Hell broth, blue ruin
Is our bosom friend
Soul destroyer, ball of fire
Turns boys into men!!
(Operatically.) To men!!

PERCY *has drained the bottle. He is staggered by the experience. It takes him a while to adjust to what has hit him. Then it seems to give him a new, wide-eyed energy.*

RAKER: Now…I should prepare for this meeting the women are holding. I have to say a few words of welcome.

SHRIKE: You're giving a speech at a Suffrage meeting?

RAKER: I'm keeping an eye on things.

SHRIKE: They're trying to overthrow three centuries of democratic tradition. They want the Vote. Why? I'll tell you why! They are strangers to joy. They are supressing natural instincts, and those instincts are breaking into flame. They are burning, burning inside. This is a frontier. There are thousands of men...decent, lusty men everywhere. But these women will not open themselves to what surrounds them. It's there. Oh, yes. It awaits only the slightest invitation. The least gentle, welcoming touch! But they hold it back! And they are burning, burning, burning!! We should have had more rehearsals for the operetta, and made them play at being in charge until they were sick of it.

INK *is mesmerized.* RAKER, *pacing about, has ignored* SHRIKE. *Suddenly,* RAKER *has a flash of thought.*

RAKER: Of course! Of course! The operetta!

SHRIKE: The operetta?

RAKER: The operetta!!

SHRIKE: Burning?

PERCY: What about the operetta?

RAKER: You all remember the part where the King is passing on the Kingdom to the Prince?

ALL: Yes!

RAKER: Where those in command display the proclamation?

SHRIKE & INK: Yes!

PERCY: You could substitute the deed to the Legislative land!

RAKER: Clever boy!

PERCY: And show it to them all!

SHRIKE: Marvellous!

RAKER: Everyone will be there...all the members of the Assembly, the Premier, the Opposition.

PERCY: We'll make a public display of the land transfer right before their eyes.

INK: Whoopee!

SHRIKE: Then let them complain if they want to.

PERCY: Most inventive, Mr. Mayor.

INK: A stroke of genius, pure genius! Why didn't I think of it?

RAKER *leads them into singing "Clever, Clever Trick."*

RAKER:

What a clever, clever trick
For this imponderable fix
And it's marvellously quick
And it's masterfully slick
What a clever, clever trick
For this imponderable fix
What a trick with the deed we will do!

SHRIKE:

What a cunning, cunning plot
To cut a complicated knot

For once the land is bought
There's no way we can be caught
What a cunning, cunning plot
To cut a complicated knot
What a plot with the deed we will do!

INK:

What a double-dealing plan
If we can't do it no one can
It's astounding sleight-of-hand
From a wizard of a man
What a double-dealing plan
If we can't do it no one can
What a plan with the deed we will do!

PERCY:

What a hocus-pocus scheme
Things will not be what they seem
It'll be just like a dream
And they won't know what they've seen
What a hocus-pocus scheme
Things will not be what they seem

RAKER:

A mysteriously magical
A most amazing classical

ALL: A clever, clever trick

SHRIKE: Oh his mind is awfully quick!

ALL: Such a clever, clever trick

INK: He's astonishingly slick!

ALL:

What a clever, clever trick
A clever, clever trick
A clever, clever trick we will do!

All now sing their own verses as a round, RAKER *leading off. This ends with:*

A mysteriously magical

A most amazing classical
A clever, clever trick
(Not RAKER.) Oh his mind is awfully quick!
Such a clever, clever trick
(Not RAKER.*)* He's astonishingly slick!

What a clever, clever trick
A clever, clever trick
A clever, clever trick we will to!
What a trick...with the deed ...we will do!!

Song ends.

RAKER: Now, gentlemen! Let's rehearse what happens after we show them the deed. To arms! To arms!

RAKER *races to the umbrella stand.* RAKER *grabs a cane, throws* SHRIKE *a cane,* PERCY *a cane, and* INK *pulls out a feather duster (or an umbrella or parasol).* RAKER *faces* SHRIKE. PERCY *faces* INK.

RAKER, SHRIKE & PERCY: En garde!

INK *(seeing what he has):* Aaahhh!

INK *tries to defend himself but* PERCY *runs him through.* INK *dies.* PERCY *puts his foot on* INK*'s chest and strikes a pose.*

RAKER *(to* SHRIKE, *as they fight):* Coward! Dog! Turncoat!

SHRIKE *(to* RAKER): Double-crosser! Villain!

RAKER *runs* SHRIKE *through.* SHRIKE *dies.* RAKER *turns to* PERCY. *He flips his cane into his left hand and advances to shake* PERCY*'s hand.* PERCY *shifts his cane and extends his hand. Quickly,* RAKER *flips his cane back and runs* PERCY *through.* PERCY *stands there, astonished.*

RAKER: Die! You fool! Die!!

PERCY: What did you do that for?

RAKER: Never forget. You're in politics now. And I'm a member of the – *(pause)* ah, Liberal Party!

RAKER *pulls out the sword.* PERCY *shrieks and dies.*

Musical tag.

ALL: What a trick…with the deed…we will do!!!

Blackout.

End of ACT ONE .

ACT TWO

Scene One

The park: a different part than in Act One. There are two grassy rises on opposite sides of the stage. Offstage, NATASHA, ANYA, JEAN *and* LETITIA *start singing. They march on (down an aisle, if desired).* NATASHA *carries a picnic basket.* ANYA *carries a sign, "Votes For Women!"*

WOMEN *(singing):*

We are marching on in the fight
In the fight (in the fight)
For women's rights (for women's rights)
We are marching on in the fight
Organizing with all our might!
(Repeat. Song ends.)

JEAN *(to* ANYA): Where's the Mayor?

ANYA: Not here yet, I guess. Just go ahead.

JEAN: All right. *(Takes* LETITIA *by the arm.)* Lassie, up here. *(She leads her up one of the rises.)* Friends!! The Mayor was supposed to be here to say a few words of welcome, and I'm sure he'll find the courage to turn up soon. But first, I'd like to tell you that we're holding this meeting on the very day that the Provincial Legislative Assembly has gathered in Regina to choose our new provincial capital because we want them to know that they have an even more important choice to make in the next session! Aye, they do!! And what could be more important than the new capital, you'd like to know? Well, that is what our speaker, who had travelled all the way from Winnipeg, is ready to tell you! Friends! It is my great pleasure to introduce, and your great pleasure to welcome, Mrs. Letitia McClung!! *(To* LETITIA.) Give it to them, girl!

WOMEN *applaud.* JEAN *steps down to stand beside* ANYA. LETITIA *holds onto some papers.*

LETITIA *(unsure, nervous):* Ah…thank you very much, Jean, for your kind opening remarks. *(Reads from papers.)* Ladies and gentlemen. Friends. A subject has been assigned to me today which I cannot begin to do justice to.

If anyone in the audience laughs, LETITIA *and* JEAN *stare them down.*

But it is a subject of very great importance, which lies very near to my heart. It is the subject of the franchise. I would like to ask you to support us in gaining the franchise, in gaining the Vote for women, first, because it is our right –

Applause from the WOMEN.

And second, because it is our duty. We are as deeply interested in our country's welfare and in our country's laws as men.

WOMEN, *trying hard, applaud again.*

JEAN *(to* ANYA*):* She needs more fire!

The MEN *arrive. As* LETITIA *continues to give her speech, various conversations take place at the same time.*

LETITIA: But on this first day of July, this grand Dominion Day, all across Canada, politicians – that is, men – will be making speeches about how wonderful a country this is. Yes. They will talk about how courageous the pioneers were in settling this land, and how much the immigrants gained when they came here. They will not mention any of the problems we still have, because they do not see them as problems.

The other conversations:

SHRIKE: They've started already.

INK: That must be their speaker.

JEAN: Here the men are now.

RAKER: Well, they'll have to stop until I've said my piece.

ANYA: There's even Mr. Teesol.

JEAN: Thistle, girl, Thistle.

PERCY: Hello, Natasha.

NATASHA *(smells liquor on him):* Hello, Mr. Thistle.

PERCY *(arms around her):* Percy's the name. Percy.

RAKER *(to* ANYA): Well, I'm here.

ANYA: You're late. Letitia has already begun.

RAKER: Then stop her. I don't have time to waste standing around.

JEAN: I'm afraid we can't do that, Mr. Mayor.

RAKER: If you don't, I will.

ANYA: Oh, all right.

ANYA stands up beside LETITIA. LETITIA stops speaking.

Excuse me, Mrs. McClung. *(Pause.)* Friends. We are fortunate today to have the Mayor of the City of Regina in attendance. He wishes to say a few words. Mr. Mayor.

RAKER *gets up on other rise.*

MEN: Speech! Speech! *(They applaud throughout speech.)*

RAKER: Thank you, my friends, thank you. Now, upon this great day, this illustrious anniversary of the foundation of our great country, we must recall the toil of those men...of those men and ladies, who made this country, and this province, what it is today.

ALICE *walks on.* RAKER *does not see her yet.*

I remember well a story told to me about the days of hardship and privation, a story told to me by an old pioneer –

While RAKER *is talking,* ALICE *and* PERCY *meet.*

ALICE: Percy! There you are.

PERCY: Hello, Alice.

PERCY *tries to kiss her and she avoids it.*

ALICE: Not here, Percy. *(She smells the liquor on his breath. Loudly.)* Percy!!

RAKER *stops in mid-speech when he hears her.*

RAKER: Alice, what are you doing here?

ALICE: Percy told me to meet him.

RAKER: Did he? *(Seeing chance to leave.)* Well, now we'll all take you home. Ladies, you are welcome to your meeting.

MEN *applaud.* RAKER *moves to* ALICE *and* PERCY.

LETITIA: I assume I may begin my speech again.

INK: Sure, go ahead. Say whatever you like, we won't hear it anyway!

INK *and* SHRIKE *laugh.*

RAKER *(to* ALICE): I told you not to come here.

ALICE: But Percy said –

PERCY *(to* RAKER): That's right Mr. Mayor.

LETITIA *(to* SHRIKE): I see.

PERCY: I told her to wait for me.

LETITIA: You and your friends are afraid to hear what I have to say.

SHRIKE: Afraid?!

RAKER: Well, let's get out of here.

SHRIKE: I'm not afraid of anything!

INK: What about Moose Jaw?

SHRIKE: Shut up, Ink!

RAKER *(to* PERCY): Get Shrike and Ink.

LETITIA: That's how it looks. Of course, I know that men such as yourself aren't afraid of anything.

PERCY *moves to* SHRIKE *and* INK. *He tugs at* INK*'s arm.* ALICE *and* RAKER *argue quietly.*

INK *(shrugs* PERCY *off):* No, we're not!

LETITIA: And you're especially not afraid of a woman!

SHRIKE: That's right. I'm not afraid of any woman! Don't you wish you were a man?

LETITIA: Don't *you* wish you were?

WOMEN *laugh.* PERCY *tries to get* SHRIKE's *attention.* SHRIKE *waves him off.*

Well, then, I'll just keep talking and let you decide for yourself whether you're going to turn tail or not.

WOMEN *applaud.*

PERCY *(getting caught up too):* And what did you say your name was?

LETITIA: The name is McClung...Mrs. Nellie Letitia McClung!

JEAN: Nellie? Now that's better! Give it to them, Nellie!

PERCY: Nellie McClung?

NELLIE: Sisters! *(*WOMEN *cheer.)* And brothers! (WOMEN *laugh,* MEN *groan.)* I'm sure these gentlemen will all agree with me that it was men of vision who built this land.

SHRIKE*:* That's absolutely correct. And the men of the CPR were right in front of all the rest.

NELLIE*:* It has always been a puzzle to me, then, that these same men of vision do not see just as clearly the problems right under their noses.

INK*:* Whadaya mean?

NELLIE*:* I mean that they do not see that women of intelligence are being kept prisoners in the so-called "woman's sphere" – the nursery, the kitchen –

SHRIKE*:* The bedroom.

INK*:* Where they belong!

MEN *laugh.*

JEAN *(to* INK): Keep a civil tongue in your head!

INK: What did you say?

JEAN: I said for you to shut your mouth and behave decently!

ANYA: Jean, no.

INK: Why, you can't say that to me!

JEAN: I can, and I just did!

INK: No, you can't. You....

SHRIKE: Ink!! No!!

INK: You're fired!

JEAN: I'm what, Mr. Ink?

RAKER: Ink! *(To* INK, *aside.)* The operetta!

INK: I said, you're...you're...you're fired-up! I meant you're fired-up! You're excited!

RAKER: And he apologizes, don't you, Ink?

INK: Yes...yes, I do. I'm sorry I interrupted.

JEAN: I see. Then that's better. Go ahead, Nellie.

When JEAN *turns away,* INK *takes a quick slug from a hip flask.*

NELLIE *(to* JEAN) : Thank you.

ANYA: Congratulations, Jean.

WOMEN *applaud.*

NELLIE: Sisters! How can these men of vision be blind to all the women working long, hard hours in evil-smelling holes called "factories?" How can they be blind to all the women toiling on farms, building up the land, but having no right to the increase that results from their labours?

SHRIKE: And what's wrong with that?

ANYA: What's wrong with that, he says?

JEAN: Go on, girl, go on!

NATASHA: What would he know about work, travelling in his special CPR coach, back and forth to Moose Jaw?

SHRIKE: Back and forth to Moo...to Moo...don't say that name!

JEAN: Aye, the CPR doesn't care about the interests of ordinary folk, especially about the interests of women!

ANYA: You don't like Moose Jaw, I suppose, because it's full of people who work for the CPR. Moose Jaw isn't good enough for you!

SHRIKE: I don't want to hear any more about...about that place!

ANYA, JEAN & NATASHA: Moose Jaw! Moose Jaw! Moose Jaw!

SHRIKE: No! No! No!

NELLIE: Sisters! How can men of vision let these evils be? How can they let women slave and sicken? How can they let women be abandoned, their homes sold out from under them, unable to do anything at all in the law? How can they let older women, widows, live in poverty? How can men of vision let such powers of mind and feeling as all women possess be constrained and wasted?

INK: Women don't know how to think!

JEAN *(astounded):* I don't believe my ears!

RAKER: That's enough, Ink!

INK: I said that women –

SHRIKE & RAKER: Ink!

NELLIE *(pause. Quietly incisive):* I think, sisters...I think that men of vision *do* see these things. And I think it's to their advantage not to do anything about it. Who owns the factories, the farms, the houses? Not women!

WOMEN: No!

NELLIE: Who controls the law and Parliament to keep things as they are? Not women!

WOMEN: No!

NELLIE: Who owns the liquor trade?

WOMEN: The men! The men!!

RAKER: You don't know what you're talking about!

INK & SHRIKE *(joining in):* She doesn't know anything! Not a thing!

NELLIE: Oh, don't I? Sisters! Do you know why men of vision refuse to give us the Vote? I'll tell you why. It's because we would sweep the new broom of reform through all of their corruption! (WOMEN *cheer.)* Yes!! The Liquor Trade knows who its friends are. So do the owners of sweat-shops, the owners of land and property, the real-estate dealers, the swindlers! Their friends are politicians...politicians with carpet-bags full of double-dealing and political skulduggery! (WOMEN *applaud and cheer.)* And perhaps that, sisters...perhaps that is why there is a Dominion Day. These men of vision have Dominion and they aim to keep it!

RAKER, SHRIKE & INK: That's right!

PERCY *(moves to* ALICE): Let's get out of here.

ALICE: No.

PERCY: Alice.

ALICE: No.

NELLIE: But sisters, we will not let them! (WOMEN *cheer.)* These men of vision stand between us and a decent society, a decent world. Our way to that decent society is through political struggle. Our way to that decent world is through the Vote! We must have the Vote! (WOMEN *cheer again.)*

RAKER *(scornful):* If you're the kind of woman that'd be elected, I'd get out of politics!

MEN *laugh and cheer.*

NELLIE: You see, sisters, what a wonderfully purifying effect we could have!

WOMEN *laugh and cheer.*

And that's only one good reason why we must have the Vote!

WOMEN: The Vote! The Vote! We want the Vote!

RAKER: Now just a minute! Just a minute! Ladies! *(*WOMEN *boo.)* You don't really want the Vote! You don't really need the Vote! *(*MEN *cheer and* WOMEN *jeer.)* And you really shouldn't have the Vote! *(Cheers and jeers.)* No!! *(Begins to sing "The Vote!")*

RAKER:

Women should not have the Vote
And let me tell you why
If they do not get their way
They sit right down and cry

MEN:

Sit right down
Sit right down
Sit right down and cry!

NELLIE:

Men should not have the Vote
It simply isn't right
If they do not get their way
They go outside and fight

WOMEN:

Go outside
Go outside
Go outside and fight!

RAKER:

Women should not have the Vote
They'll break apart the home
They'll never wash, never cook
They'll let the children roam

MEN:

Womens' place
Womens' place
Womens' place is home!

NELLIE:

Men should not have the Vote
They don't know how to think
Whenever there's a problem
They just have another drink

WOMEN:

Have another
Have another
Have another drink!

ALL MEN:

Women should not have the Vote
They don't know what it's for
They're absolutely ignorant
Of Parliamentary lore
Parliamentary
Parliamentary
Parliamentary lore!

WOMEN: Men should not have the Vote!

MEN: Women should not have the Vote!

WOMEN: Men should not have the Vote!

MEN: Women should not have the Vote!

ALL:

Men (Women) should not have the Vote
The world will go to hell
You don't know what you're doing
You don't even do that well
Don't do that, don't do that
Don't even do that well!

There is nothing you can say
Will make us think we're wrong
You know what we say is true
You've known it all along
It's the Vote, it's the Vote
You know we should have the Vote
You've known it all along!
It's the Vote, it's the Vote
Yes, it is, it's the Vote
The Vote that makes us strong!!

Both groups cheer and raise a ruckus.

RAKER: I've heard enough of this!

INK *(petulant):* Let's have our own meeting!

The WOMEN *crowd around* NELLIE, *congratulating her.*

WOMEN: That was wonderful, Nellie, wonderful! *(Etc.)*

RAKER *(to* WOMEN): You all better be at the operetta tonight.

ANYA: Don't worry, we will be.

RAKER: Natasha! This was one of your errands, was it? Bring along that picnic basket and serve us lunch right now.

ANYA *(protecting* NATASHA) : That is our basket.

ANYA *takes the basket.*

JEAN: Nellie McClung! Now that's a name with punch! You might even be famous one day!

NELLIE *laughs.* JEAN *leads the* WOMEN *in singing a reprise of "We Are Marching" and they march around the stage.* ALICE *has picked up the sign, and follows them. They are about to go off.*

PERCY: Alice!

RAKER: Natasha!

ALICE *and* NATASHA *stop, as does* ANYA. JEAN *and* NELLIE *exit.*

ANYA: What do you want my daughter for, Mr. Mayor?

RAKER: To make us some lunch.

ANYA: Are you men so helpless?

RAKER: I've wasted a lot of time here because of your invitation. We have some very important business problems to deal with.

NATASHA: It's all right, mother. I'll make lunch for Mr. Raker.

ANYA: As you wish.

ALICE *(to* ANYA): And I'd like to talk with Mrs. McClung...may I go with you?

ANYA: A fair trade, Mr. Mayor?

PERCY: No, it's not. Alice, you were going to have lunch with me.

NATASHA: I'll make your lunch as well.

ANYA *(to* RAKER): What do you say, Mr. Mayor?

RAKER *(reluctant, but operating under constraints the others don't know about):* She can go if she wants.

PERCY *(moves to* ALICE): I thought you weren't interested in the Vote?

ALICE: I wasn't.

PERCY *(grabs her arm):* Then don't waste your time with that mob.

ALICE *(astonished at his action):* Let me go!

PERCY: I have something to tell you.

ALICE *(under her breath):* Percy, you've been drinking! Let me go! *(Pulls away. Starts to go with* ANYA.)

PERCY: At least don't forget we have to practice our duet for the operetta.

ANYA *and* ALICE *go off.*

RAKER: Natasha.

NATASHA: Yes, sir.

RAKER: Go back to the house and pack a picnic lunch for us.

NATASHA: Certainly, sir.

NATASHAS *exits.*

SHRIKE: A picnic lunch? Why don't we eat in a civilized fashion, inside your house? Get away from the dreadful smell of this marsh.

RAKER: I thought you liked the smell of money, Mr. Shrike?

INK: The smell of money?

SHRIKE: I smell the marsh, not the money, Mr. Mayor.

RAKER: The marsh smells like money to me, Mr. Shrike.

INK: Ah! Of course!

PERCY *(annoyed, looking after* ALICE): If I'd known she was going to treat me like this….

SHRIKE *(falsely consoling):* Mr. Thistle, you'll soon find that women are more trouble than they're worth. Perhaps you'd like to reconsider.

INK: Yes, damn women anyway!

RAKER: I need a good cigar and a drink...by God, a good drink!

SHRIKE: One of the necessities of the civilized life...*(Pulls out a silver hip flask)*...Your pleasure, sir.

RAKER: Thank you, Mr. Shrike. *(He drinks.)* Anyway gentlemen, don't worry. We're still the ones in control.

RAKER *drinks again, then leads them in singing "Men, Men, Men." During the course of the song, they work themselves into a fit of Ukrainian dancing, ending up exhausted.*

RAKER *(passing flask back to* SHRIKE, *who drinks. Sings):*

They want to run for Parliament
They'd love to be the Government
But Votes are not from Heaven sent
No, Votes belong to men

ALL:

Men, men, men, men, Votes belong to men, to men
To men, men, men, men, Votes belong to men!

SHRIKE *(passes flask to* INK, who drinks) :

They're just like bears who want some honey
When they think about our money
Without money no one's free
But banks belong to men

ALL:

Men, men, men, men, Banks belong to men, to men
Oh men, men, men, men, Banks belong to men!

INK *(passes flask to* PERCY, *who drinks):*

It's clear to any kind of fool
The law gives us the right to rule
We're the masters, they're the tools
Cause Judges all are men

ALL:

Men, men, men, men, Judges all are men, are men
Oh men, men, men, men, Judges all are men!

PERCY:

Both old and new philosophy

Anatomy, psychology
And history, theology
All give control to men

ALL:

So ladies stay where you belong
We know what's right, we know what's wrong
Remember we are smart and strong
Because we are the men!
Men, men, men, men, yes we are the men, the men
Oh men, men, men, men, yes we are the men!
Men, men, men, men, yes we are the men, the men
Oh men, men, men, men, yes we are the men!
Hey!!!

Song ends.

RAKER: Now let's take a look at the marsh. I'm sure Natasha will find us there.

PERCY: I'll wait and show her the way.

RAKER: Fine, my boy, fine. Gentlemen.

He leads SHRIKE *and* INK *off.*

SHRIKE: If that Mrs. Burke thinks she can shout Moo...shout Moo...shout at me and still keep working at the CPR, she is mistaken.

RAKER: No, no, Shrike. You don't have to bother about things like that. She's not dangerous.

INK *(fuming):* Maybe she isn't, but we should run that Nellie McClung out of town. She's preaching the overthrow of the established order. It's seduction, that's what it is! Seduction!

SHRIKE: You mean sedition, Ink, sedition!

INK: I do?

They exit.

PERCY *sits down at the bench. He still has the flask. He takes a pull.*

PERCY *(sings):*

So ladies stay where you belong
We know what's right, we know what's wrong
Remember we are smart and – *(Groans.)*

No sleep, thirty cups of tea, seven pieces of saskatoon pie... *(Considers flask.)*...and now this. *(He tips flask and drains it.)* Everything's happening so fast. Fifty thousand dollars. Fifty thousand dollars! I could go back to Saskatoon and buy *The Phoenix* ...turn it into a real newspaper. But when Alice and I – *(As if realizing this for the first time.)* – when I get married to Alice, then I'll have to move to British Columbia. What am I doing? And then, just when I'm going to tell her the news, she goes off with those women. Isn't this just what she wanted? *(Shakes head and holds it in his hands.)* Things keep spinning around.

NATASHA *returns, carrying a picnic basket. She sees him sitting there. He does not notice her. She walks quietly up beside him.*

NATASHA: Percy?

PERCY *(startled):* What?! Oh...it's you. What are you sneaking up on me for?

NATASHA *(sets basket on bench):* Are you all right?

PERCY *(getting unreasonably angry):* Sure. I feel...I feel just great! Why shouldn't I? Alice runs off just when I'm about to tell her we can get married.

NATASHA: Married?! *(Hopes shattered.)* Oh.

PERCY: Yes, married. It's all arranged.

NATASHA: All arranged.

PERCY: Why did she go?

NATASHA: What?

PERCY: Why did Alice go off with those women?

NATASHA: I don't know.

PERCY: Well, you *should* know. Your mother believes in this stuff. I guess you believe in it too.

NATASHA: Yes, I do.

PERCY: Then tell me. *(Takes her arm.)* Tell me why she went.

NATASHA: Percy, please let me go.

PERCY: Not until you tell me. *(Holds both her arms.)* You asked me here. You wanted me to do a story.

NATASHA: You've been drinking.

PERCY: You can't tell me, can you?

NATASHA: You heard Nellie McClung as well as I did. You heard her say that women are constrained by the rule of men.

PERCY: I don't believe that.

NATASHA: Don't you? Then what are you doing now?

PERCY: Trying to get a straight answer.

NATASHA: Percy, let me go.

PERCY: I have to know.

NATASHA: You're hurting me.

PERCY *(shakes her):* Tell me. Come on, tell me!

He stops shaking her. They look at each other. They kiss. After a long moment NATASHA *breaks away and starts to cry.*

NATASHA: Go away. You don't know what you're doing.

PERCY *(gives her his handkerchief):* Here. Take this. *(Picks up basket.)* Better get this to the men. All right? *(Starts to move off.)* All right?

PERCY *takes the basket and walks off, staggering a bit.* NATASHA *sits on the ground, dabbing her eyes with the handkerchief.*

NATASHA *(angered and upset):* Getting married.

From offstage, we hear ANYA *and* ALICE *singing the last verse of "The Vote" and laughing. They enter.*

ALICE: Mrs. McClung is a wonderful woman!

ANYA: Yes, she is.

ALICE: I'd love to talk to her for hours.

They see NATASHA. *They hurry to her side. She is not so much hurt as angry.*

ANYA: Natasha, *daragaichka*, what's the matter?

NATASHA: I'll be all right. *(Blows her nose.)*

ANYA: What happened?

NATASHA: It's nothing. I...I fell down.

ANYA: You fell?

NATASHA: I was hurrying with the lunch.

ALICE: I'll take it to them. *(Looks around for the basket.)*

NATASHA: They...they've got it already.

ALICE *(puzzled):* Oh.

ANYA: They were waiting here? Why didn't they help you back to the house?

NATASHA: I said it was nothing. *(Cries some more.)*

ANYA: Then why are you still crying like this?

NATASHA *(crying):* I don't know.

ALICE *(sees the handkerchief):* Natasha, why do you have Percy's handkerchief?

NATASHA: He didn't mean anything. He's been drinking.

ANYA: There must be something going on with those men.

NATASHA: He wanted to know why you went away with Mrs. McClung. He...he grabbed my arms.

ALICE *(surprised, angry):* He what? He grabbed your arms?

ANYA: You should not be so surprised. Property. That is all we are to those men. Our struggle to have a voice threatens them, threatens this system they have created. It frightens them, and so they try to frighten us, try to tell us "Do not dare!". They like cheap labour in their offices and factories. They like to be able to marry a woman and have her work for nothing in the home. These men, these owners and masters, they like it this way!

ALICE: I don't know...men have always been courteous to me.

ANYA: You have had time to make yourself pretty. You have never had to work for a living – *(Stops.)* I am sorry. It's not your fault.

NATASHA: He was angry because he wanted to tell you –

ALICE: Tell me what?

NATASHA *(crying again):* That you can...that you can get married.

ALICE *(amazed):* My father agreed?!

NATASHA *(crying harder):* Yes.

ANYA *(comforts* NATASHA*)*: There, there *daragaichka.*

ALICE: We can get married? *(Not sure she really wants this any more.)*

NATASHA: Yes.

ALICE: But Natasha, what's the matter now?

NATASHA *(sobs louder):* I'm happy for you.

ALICE: I see. *(She does see.)* You're in love with him, aren't you? I thought so.

ANYA: Love...love is so difficult. You think you love someone, you tell them, and then....You have to be so careful with love, and love will not let you be careful. Once I loved a man, but then he changed. *(Sings.)*

Never seek to tell your love
Love that never told can be
For the gentle wind does move
Silently, invisibly
For the gentle wind does move
Silently, invisibly

I told my love, I told my love
I told him all my heart

And once he had heard my love
He tore it apart

ALL:

Never seek to tell your love
Love that never told can be
For the gentle wind does move
Silently, invisibly

ANYA:

For the gentle wind does move
Silently, invisibly

Now that he has gone from me
I'm left to wonder why
How silently, invisibly
The wind may wander by

ALL:

Never seek to tell your love
Love that never told can be
For the gentle wind does move
Silently, invisibly
For the gentle wind does move
Silently, invisibly

From far off, PERCY *calls.*

PERCY *(off):* Natasha? Natasha?

ALICE: It's Percy.

ANYA *(to* NATASHA): I'll take you home.

ALICE: No. Hide over there. Please wait.

ANYA: All right.

ANYA *and* NATASHA *go off.*

PERCY *(closer):* Natasha? *(He enters. He is pretty drunk.)*

ALICE: Yes, Percy?

PERCY: Oh... Alice. I thought you were with that McClung woman.

ALICE: And I thought you were with my father.

PERCY: I was. He's coming along soon.

ALICE: I see. And what did you want with Natasha?

PERCY: Oh, nothing. *(Switches subject.)* So you really don't want the Vote?

ALICE: I was curious, that's all.

PERCY: That's okay, then. *(Comes closer.)* Alice.

ALICE: Yes?

PERCY: Sweetheart, I've got some wonderful news.

ALICE: Some news?

PERCY: Yes. Your father's agreed to let us get married.

ALICE: He has, has he?

PERCY: And I'm getting some money. Enough money to move to British Columbia and set up my own paper. You see. Everything you wanted.

ALICE: Of course. Everything I wanted.

PERCY: Alice. *(Tries to embrace her. She holds him at arms' length.)*

ALICE: Uh huh?

ALICE *has begun to cry.*

PERCY: Tears of happiness, hey? Here, take my – *(Goes to pull out handkerchief, and it isn't there.)(Sings.)*

Every time I fall asleep
And dreams go floating round
Your face is all I see
Your voice the only sound
Oh my darling what can I do
Unless you're with me in daytime too?

ALICE *(aside):*

Can I be sure these aren't lies
Or are you wearing a disguise?

PERCY:

Every time the morning sun
Flows across my bed
On the pillow next to me
I see your lovely head
Oh my darling what can I do
Unless you're with me in night-time too?
Why are there tears in your eyes?

ALICE *(aside):* Can I be sure these aren't lies?

PERCY: Can't you see my love has no disguise?

ALICE *(aside):* Or are you wearing a disguise?

Song ends.

The other men enter. INK *carries the empty picnic basket.* RAKER *and* SHRIKE *are rather drunk,* INK *is soused.*

RAKER: Well, what's this, what's this?

SHRIKE: I thought he stole off after her.

INK: Better luck next time, Shrike.

SHRIKE *(the gloves):* Shut up, Ink.

PERCY: I've told Alice you agreed to let us marry.

ALICE: No, wait –

RAKER *(to* ALICE): And of course you said yes…it's just what you wanted. Congratulations, my boy.

INK: When do I get to kiss the bride?

RAKER: Later, Ink, later.

ALICE: Father, really –

RAKER: We can announce the engagement this evening.

PERCY: After the operetta.

RAKER *(an idea):* No! As part of the operetta!

PERCY: Right after the courtship!

RAKER: Exactly. And right before the wedding scene.

SHRIKE: A preview of the real occasion. Ha!

RAKER: It will attract attention away from the land transfer.

SHRIKE: The public transfer of your daughter, Mr. Mayor, will disguise the public transfer of the deed to the land.

INK: Money, money, money! Here we come! I'm going to be a judge! A judge!!

SHRIKE: And I can kiss goodbye to…to…you know where.

PERCY: And we can move to British Columbia and I can set up my own paper.

RAKER: And the Government can have a wonderful site overlooking Wascana Marsh for its new Legislature. Well, everything works our fine. Come along, gentlemen, this calls for a real celebration! Percy! *(Arm around shoulder.)* Son.

PERCY: Yes, Father?

All the men start to leave.

INK *(passing* ALICE, *hands her the basket):* Here. *(Burps.)* You can carry this.

PERCY *(calls back):* Alice.

ALICE: I'll be along soon.

PERCY: Okay. I'll see you at the house then.

ANYA *and* NATASHA *enter.* NATASHA *has stopped crying. She gives* ALICE *the handkerchief to wipe her tears.* ALICE *starts to use it and then throws it to the ground.*

ALICE: You heard?

NATASHA: Yes.

ANYA: Everything. I knew they were up to something.

ALICE: I don't know what to do.

ANYA: Do you want to marry him?

ALICE: I don't know. I thought I loved him. But maybe I just hated Mr. Shrike.

ANYA: I see.

ALICE *(to* NATASHA): And do you still love him?

NATASHA: I think so. Yes.

ALICE: What are we going to do? I'll have to marry him.

ANYA: No, there may be a way out.

ALICE: What do you mean?

ANYA: The operetta.

NATASHA: The operetta?

ALL: The operetta!

Music vamp.

They exit. NATASHA *picks up the handkerchief. Instrumental reprise as the lights on the stage go down. Lights stay up on* PIANO PLAYER. *A stagehand enters, carrying capes or other costume pieces for the operetta. The* PIANO PLAYER *puts on the cape. Music for "Magic Reversals" begins. The lights rise slowly on the rest of the stage. This is the stage of the theatre where the operetta will be performed. The "curtain" is down. Stagehands are dressing the set. This includes swords on the walls. As the music ends,* INK *and* SHRIKE *enter, and we are into:*

SCENE TWO

INK *(peeks out imaginary curtain, and shrieks):* Aaaahhh!

SHRIKE: What's the matter?

INK: There's people out there! *(Takes a slug from flask.)*

SHRIKE: Of course there's people. It's the audience for the operetta.

INK: I've never acted in front of an audience before.

SHRIKE: I thought lawyers did that all the time.

INK: I never take a case that has to go to court. *(He drinks.)*

SHRIKE: And you want to be a judge?! Get hold of yourself! Are you sure you remember what you're supposed to do?

INK: Remember? Of course I remember. *(Drinks.)*

SHRIKE *(the gloves):* Stop that! What is it, then?

INK: When the King...

SHRIKE: Yes.

INK: When the King is passing on the Kingdom to the Prince....

SHRIKE: Yes.

INK *(panic):* I show everybody the transfer!

SHRIKE *(the gloves):* No! No! No!

INK: We don't show the transfer?

SHRIKE: When the King....

INK: Yes.

SHRIKE: Is passing on the Kingdom to the Prince....

INK: Yes.

SHRIKE: And giving the proclamation of transfer to all of us to examine....

INK: Yes.

SHRIKE: We substitute the transfer to the Legislature land.

INK: Aha! Then I show it to everybody!

SHRIKE: Yes! Now, do you have our transfer?

INK: No. Yes. Right...*(He begins to search his pockets.)*

SHRIKE: Ink!

INK *(finds it at last):* Right here!

SHRIKE: And are you sure you know what you're supposed to do?

INK: When the King....

SHRIKE: Yes.

INK: Is passing on the Kingdom to the Prince....

SHRIKE: Yes.

INK *(pause):* Could we go through it one more time?

SHRIKE *(the gloves):* Ink!!!

SHRIKE *sees that* ANYA, NATASHA *and* JEAN *are about to come on stage.*

SHRIKE*:* It's the women! Put that transfer away and let's get out of here!

They rush off. JEAN, ANYA *and* NATASHA *enter.*

JEAN: Is Nellie ready?

ANYA: I don't know.

NATASHA: She's with Alice.

JEAN: Well, she better be prepared. Mr. Shrike and Mr. Ink have arrived.

ANYA: Why don't you go and see?

JEAN: Aye. It looks like I should.

JEAN *goes off.* RAKER *strides on, crossing the stage.* ANYA, *with* NATASHA *at her side, confronts him.*

ANYA: I must speak with you.

RAKER: Not here! Not now! *(Looks around.)*

ANYA: I have something important to discuss.

INK, *in union suit, rushes onto stage.*

INK: Where's my costume?! *(Stops.)* Have you seen my costume? *(Not waiting.)* Who took my costume?

INK *rushes out the way he has come in.*

RAKER: I have to get into my costume.

ANYA: It is about my daughter.

RAKER: We'll talk about it later...after the performance.

RAKER *starts to exit.* ANYA *follows.*

ANYA: You promise?

RAKER: I promise.

As RAKER *and* ANYA *exit,* ALICE *enters, wearing an elaborate gown.*

NATASHA: Is Nellie ready?

ALICE: Yes, Jean's guarding her.

NATASHA: So you'll still do the Prologue?

ALICE: Yes. And you'll take my part after that. You know the script.

NATASHA: Yes. And the other costume?

ALICE: Is in the dressing room.

NATASHA: And then you'll take my role later?

ALICE: Yes.

NATASHA: And you've got the contracts?

ALICE: Jean prepared them. She swears they'll stand up in any court.

NATASHA: They only have to be signed?

ALICE: Yes.

PERCY *(off):* Alice? Alice?

ALICE: Quick!

NATASHA *dashes off.* ALICE *remains where she is.* PERCY *comes in wearing the costume of a prince. He has a dreadful hangover. He looks green.*

PERCY: Where have you been?

ALICE: The curtain's about to go up.

PERCY: I thought you were going to follow me home.

ALICE: You don't look very well, Percy. You really ought to get some sleep.

PERCY: I did fall asleep. And I woke up with this horrible headache.

The Overture begins with a resounding chord.

PERCY: Ooh! Stop that noise!

From offstage, a panic. SHRIKE *runs across the stage,* INK *trailing.*

SHRIKE: The cake! Where's the wedding cake?!

RAKER *strides on. He has put on his chain of office.*

RAKER *(to* ALICE): Where have you been?

ALICE: The curtain's about to go up.

RAKER: Ah, yes. Get off for a moment. I have to make a speech.

ALICE *and* PERCY *leave, in opposite directions.* RAKER *beckons to the backstage and the "curtain" goes up, i.e., a spot on* RAKER. *All backstage applaud. The Overture stops, haltingly.*

RAKER: Premier Scott, Gentlemen of the Legislative Assembly, Honoured guests, ladies. On behalf of the noble City of which I have the privilege and pleasure to be Mayor ... *(Backstage applause.)*... thank you, thank you...I say, on behalf of this noble City, Queen of the Western Plains, and soon, I hope, to be the Queen of the Province itself...on behalf of citizens and City Council of Regina I would like to welcome you all to this special performance of the operetta "Magic Reversals." I hardly need remind you of the fuss certain women are raising all across the prairies about getting the Vote. How much better if they would only continue to keep that place they now adorn – truly a higher place – and remain gentle and pure...an inspiration to those of us who have to struggle with the harsh realities of this world. And now – let the play begin!! Maestro!!

The Overture begins again. The lights dim. ALICE *and* PERCY *rush on and take their places. The "curtain" rises, i.e., the lights go up. The* PIANO PLAYER *plays recitative chords.*

PERCY *(romantic style):* What a truly magnificent day here in our most beautiful land! Do you hear those lovely melodies of birds? *(They listen.)* Of birds?

They listen. After a moment, bird songs (from the PIANO PLAYER*'s bird whistle) start up abruptly, then stop suddenly.*

ALICE *(shouting in* PERCY's ear) : Oh, yes, Prince, I do!

PERCY *(backs off):* That today beyond all other days should be the most gorgeous day of the year is indeed propitious.

ALICE *(shouts):* Verily, it is!

PERCY: For, look you, today is the day of our great annual festival.

ALICE: When upon the seventh day of the seventh month....

PERCY: As the moon riseth full in the darkening sky....

ALICE: Then do those who have power....

PERCY *(speeds it up to get it over with):* Surrender it freely....

ALICE: To those who have none....

PERCY: For all of the night....

ALICE: To rule as they wish....

PERCY: And this magic time....

ALICE: Begins with a dance....

BOTH: So let evening come! *(They beckon to the sky.)*

The lights drop abruptly down to dark. ALICE *and* PERCY *go off.*

PERCY: Did you have to shout?

The lights go up again. ANYA *and* JEAN *come in dressed in splendid male costumes as King and General.* SHRIKE *tiptoes on.* INK *is thrown on.* RAKER *makes a grand entrance. The* MEN *are dressed in marvelous long dresses. The* WOMEN *have swords on their waists. The*

MEN *carry fans. After a waltz intro, they all dance and sing "The Magic Reversals Waltz."*

MEN *(sing):* For tonight only we give you this power!

WOMEN: Thank you so much, we thank you!

MEN: It's your turn to rule for at least several hours!

WOMEN: Thank you so much, we thank you!

ALL:

It's a tradition both ancient and wise
That allows us – by law – to appear in this guise

(Chorus.) Magic Reversals (Magic Reversals)
Nothing is quite what it seems
(What it seems to be)
Magic Reversals (Magic Reversals)
You're in the world of a dream

It may seem to you that we're topsy-turvy
Don't know where we're going from
(Where we're going from)
Backwards is forwards, forwards is upwards
Oh but we have so much fun! Ha! Ha! Ha!

Repeat chorus, then:

RAKER: I'm really the King.

ANYA: But now I'm Her Majesty.

RAKER: Just for tonight!

ANYA: I have the power.

SHRIKE: And I am the General.

JEAN: He was the General. Now I'm the General.

SHRIKE: For a few hours.

ALL:

Magic Reversals (Magic Reversals)
Nothing is quite what it seems

(What it seems to be)
Magic Reversals (Magic Reversals)
It may look radical
But it's so classical
There's nothing tragical
It's really magical
Magical, magical, magical, magical,
Magical, magical, Magic Reversals!!

They stop singing and dancing. The WOMEN *bow. The* MEN *curtsy and fan themselves.* NATASHA *enters, dressed in princely garb. She has* PERCY*'s handkerchief in her pocket. Music sting.*

MEN: The Prince! *(They see it isn't* ALICE.) The Prince??!

JEAN *bows to* NATASHA. ANYA, *the King, does not.*

NATASHA: Your Majesty. *(She bows.)* I am your most devoted servant.

INK *(behind fan, to* SHRIKE): But Alice is supposed to be the Prince!

SHRIKE *(whaps him with fan):* I know that!

Music sting as PERCY *enters, dressed as the belle of the ball. He sees the Prince, does a double-take, then falls into a swoon.*

SHRIKE: Oh dear, cast your eyes upon a pitiful sight!

RAKER: Poor child, the Commoner hath fallen into a swoon at the figure of the Prince.

They rush to him.

PERCY *(under breath, to* RAKER): What's going on? Where's Alice?

RAKER: I don't know.

INK: Verily, I say, do you think he will entice her gaze to fall upon him?

RAKER: No man hath yet reached her heart. Forsooth, it is locked inside the castle called Indifference, guarded by the dark moat of Carelessness.

PERCY *(awakening):* Oh, where am I? Where am I? My poor eyes hath beheld such a vision! *(He looks around.)* And yes! Yes! They do behold it again! *(He falls into another swoon.)*

JEAN *(to* ANYA): Marry, these men be spin-brain fools!

NATASHA: They be comely though. Regard yon swooner's nether limbs.

ANYA: You rake! Tis not his nether limbs you long to rest your gaze upon!

The WOMEN *guffaw.* PERCY *wakes.*

SHRIKE *(to* PERCY): There be only one path to a woman's heart.

PERCY: How now, how now, I know, I know!

INK: You must charm her...be innocent and helpless and pretty.

RAKER: Yes, go thither. Show yourself off.

PERCY: Oh, I would that I could. Yet every time I look at her it is as if my insides were filled with a tangle of butterflies that flit and flit about. How strong, how comely she is!

SHRIKE: You must be falling –

PERCY *begins to swoon again.*

SHRIKE: Not like that!

RAKER: Falling in love.

PERCY: Oh, yes, forsooth, I am...falling in love!

Music for "Love (Times Nine) Song" begins.

PERCY *(sings, uneasily):*

Oh I love you
With a love so true
So let me, do
Sing my song for you

ALL MEN:

It's a love, love, love, love, love, love, love, love, love song!
It's a love, love, love, love, love, love, love, love, love song!
It's a love (PERCY *holds "love" while the other* MEN sing all nine)
song!

NATASHA:

How your cheeks do glow

When you sing it so
With your voice so low

How can I say no?
To your –

WOMEN *sing chorus.*

PERCY & NATASHA:

When I look at you
I feel love so true
It's just me and you
In a dream come true!

ALL *sing chorus romantically and excessively. Song ends.*

NATASHA *(to* ANYA*):* Oh, your Majesty, I think I have fallen in love too.

ANYA*:* That is too bad…the chit is only a churl.

INK *(behind fan):* What did she say?

SHRIKE *(behind fan):* Shut up!

JEAN*:* Forsooth, no-one knows what he is. He was discovered on his doorstep *(Points to* RAKER.) one dark and stormy night.

RAKER: Verily, it was a dark and stormy morning.

JEAN: Speak when you're spoken to!

RAKER: Sorry, your Magnificence.

JEAN: Let's examine him, Your Majesty, before deciding.

They walk over to PERCY.

ANYA: Prithee, churl, can you cook and sew and wash floors and make beds?

PERCY *(demure):* Yes, Your Highness.

RAKER: Yea, I taught him all those things myself.

JEAN: Silence!

NATASHA: He hath a gallant form.

The WOMEN *surround* PERCY.

ANYA: Let's have a closer look. *(To* JEAN.) Seize him.

JEAN *grabs* PERCY *by the arms from behind.*

PERCY *(under his breath):* What are you doing?

ANYA *(to* NATASHA): And this is truly the one you want?

NATASHA: Yes, Your Highness.

SHRIKE (to RAKER): What's going on?

RAKER: I don't know.

PERCY *(under breath):* Please let me go.

ANYA *(shouts in ear):* Not until you tell me...tell me why you wish to marry the Prince!

PERCY *(under breath):* This isn't in the script!

ANYA *(shouts):* Surely you can tell me that!

JEAN *(shouts):* Go ahead! Tell Her Majesty!

PERCY: My head! You're hurting me!

JEAN *(shouts):* Then tell us. Come on, tell us!

She shakes him again.

Answer Her Majesty!

PERCY *(tries to twist away. It hurts):* Ouch!

NATASHA: Are you crying, my sweet? Tears of happiness, hey?

NATASHA *dabs his eyes with the handkerchief, then puts it in his bodice.*

PERCY *(understanding):* Oh. Then all of you know ...?!

ANYA *(to* JEAN): Let him go. *(To* NATASHA.) You know he's only a commoner.

NATASHA: Commoner or not, I want him.

ANYA: Then you shall have him. And, when you marry, you shall also have his kingdom.

JEAN: You can't abdicate, Your Majesty! Forsooth, you know how your subjects love you. *(Indicates* MEN, *who do not respond.* JEAN *repeats.)* Forsooth, you know how much your subjects love you! *(And makes sure* MEN *smile and curtsy.)*

ANYA: No, I have had enough of Kinging. *(To* NATASHA.) It is your turn now.

NATASHA: Why, Your Grace....

ANYA: Protest no more. I have already had the proclamation prepared. General?

INK *(behind fan):* It's the proclamation!

SHRIKE *(behind fan):* I know!

RAKER *(to* INK): You have the deed of transfer?

INK: The transfer?! The transfer?!

INK *searches himself frantically.*

SHRIKE: You put it down here!

SHRIKE *fishes it out of* INK*'s bodice, along with his flask.* INK *takes a drink.*

JEAN *(produces the proclamation from a table):* Here, Your Omnipotence.

She unrolls it and hands it to ANYA *with a pen.*

ANYA: I thank you heartily. *(Signs it with a flourish.)* Let the people see it.

JEAN: Certainly. *(She takes it to the* MEN.)

JEAN *walks away, as the men exchange the proclamation for the deed to the land.*

RAKER *(to* INK): Display it to the audience, Ink.

INK: Of course!

INK *goes wild, running around the stage, waving the transfer in the air.*

Look at this! Look at this! It's a deed of transfer!

SHRIKE: Not like that, you fool!

The WOMEN *are consulting. As* INK *passes them, they surround him and grab the transfer.*

INK: What?! What are you doing?!

ANYA: Sorry, that was a proclamation for exterminating rats! (WOMEN *shuffle papers.)* This is the real proclamation.

INK: This isn't it!

NATASHA *(holds up another):* Or is this it?

INK: This isn't it!

JEAN *(holds up another):* Isn't this the one you wanted, Your Majesty?

INK: This isn't it!

The WOMEN *shuffle papers. The* MEN *are aghast.* INK *scurries from one* WOMAN *to the other, trying to find the real deed of transfer. They keep handing him proclamations, none of them what he wants.*

SHRIKE *(to* RAKER): This isn't in the script either.

RAKER: They must know about the land.

ANYA *holds the deed up.* INK *tries to go for it.* JEAN *and* NATASHA *ward him off with drawn swords. The music halts.*

ANYA: Right. This is it. *(To* INK.) Bring on the wedding cake.

INK *(grudgingly):* The cake? Bah!

They motion him with swords, and he goes off. He returns, pushing a huge wedding cake with (unknown to INK) NELLIE MCCLUNG *hidden inside, dressed in a suitable costume, possibly an Admiral.*

ANYA: Now General, Prince...I'll need you to witness this. Then we can bring on the Archbishop and get on with the nuptial rites.

The WOMEN *gather round the deed and busy themselves signing it.*

PERCY: What are we going to do?

SHRIKE: We have to stop them!

RAKER: We better get to the end of the play – forget the wedding. We can't let them do anything more. Let's take our power back right now!

They signal the PIANO PLAYER *to play "Revolution." He begins. The* MEN *sing. The* WOMEN *pretend not to notice.*

MEN:

This is all, all, all a dreadful mistake
A dreadful mistake!
It's a most, most, most unnatural state
Unnatural state!
This is all, all, all a dreadful mistake
A dreadful mistake!
It's their hold over us that we must break!

So we must have a revolution
It's the only real solution
To reverse this misdirection
We must start an insurrection
We must have a revolution
It's the only real solution
To correct this unnatural state!

Song ends.

MEN: To Arms! To Arms!

They grab the swords from the wall.

JEAN *(shouts):* A revolt!

The WOMEN *pull out their swords.*

PERCY *(holding his head):* No noise. Please, no noise. *(He gingerly takes a sword.)*

RAKER *squares off with* ANYA, SHRIKE *with* NATASHA, INK *with* JEAN. JEAN *makes short work of him, then turns to* PERCY. PERCY *winces at the sound of the swords striking.* INK *crawls into the corner and has a drink. The* MEN *drive the* WOMEN *back to the platform on which the cake is sitting. At last it appears that they have subdued the* WOMEN. ANYA *ends up on the platform, standing beside the cake. The* WOMEN *surrender their swords.* INK *is summoned to hold them.*

RAKER: All right. Where is it? Which one of you has it?

ANYA *(pulls it out):* Is this what you want?

RAKER *steps on the platform as* ANYA *backs off it. At this moment,* NELLIE MCCLUNG *bursts out of the top of the cake. She is singing at the top of her lungs.*

NELLIE*:* Waaaaiiiiitttttt!!!!!!!

RAKER *leaps off the platform, screaming, into the arms of* SHRIKE *and* PERCY. INK *drops the swords and the* WOMEN *grab them all back. They whistle the swords through the air, surround* NELLIE, *and confront the* MEN. ANYA *hands the deed up to* NELLIE. NELLIE *holds it aloft.* RAKER *is set on his feet.*

INK: It's the deed!

INK *moves to try and grab it, but the swords ward him off.*

ANYA: Now, Mr. Mayor, what were you about to say?

RAKER: Well....

NELLIE: Friends! What the Mayor was about to tell us is that he and his comrades *(Indicates other* MEN.) support the Vote for women!

SHRIKE & INK: We do not!!

NELLIE: That's what this document says. Or perhaps you'd like me to read from it directly?

RAKER: No...no. We agree...that's what it says.

NELLIE: That all of you support the Vote for women?

ANYA, JEAN & NATASHA: Right?

MEN *(mumble):* Right.

WOMEN: What's that?

MEN *(louder):* Right.

WOMEN: Votes for Women!!

They indicate the MEN *should join in.*

MEN*:* Votes for Women.

WOMEN: Louder!

MEN *(shout):* Votes for Women!!

NELLIE: And what's more, my friends, they're planning to make a generous contribution to our campaign!

WOMEN *cheer.* MEN *mumble.*

NELLIE: Quite a large contribution!

WOMEN *cheer wildly.*

NELLIE *(quietly to* MEN): Fifty per cent isn't too much to ask, is it gentlemen?

INK: That's a hundred thou –

SHRIKE *(the fan):* Ink!!

RAKER: Oh no, fifty per cent is very reasonable, very reasonable.

SHRIKE: Now I'll never get out of Moo...out of Moo...out of Mooo....

INK: Shut up, Shrike!

NELLIE: Well. A contribution of one hundred thousand dollars. Thank you very much indeed, gentlemen. *(To audience.)* And thank all of you for being witnesses to the generosity of the Mayor and his colleagues! And now, on with the play! *(She beckons.)* Archbishop!

The PIANO PLAYER *begins to play the wedding march.* ALICE *enters, dressed as the Archbishop. All the* MEN *curtsy. All the* WOMEN *bow.*

PERCY: Oh no, it's Alice.

ALICE *moves to the platform.* NATASHA *moves to stand in front of her.* JEAN *escorts* PERCY *to stand near* NATASHA.

ALICE: Dearly beloved, we are all gathered here to witness the joining in holy bonds of matrimony of this Prince and this commoner. Verily I say unto you that marriage is an honourable estate and should not be entered into lightly. In sooth, it would be best should both parties have a trust complete in their betrothed. To this end, and knowing well the purity of the heart of the Prince, the King hath required me to perform a Ceremony of Purification for this commoner, that he may be purged of all his sins, in thought, in word, in deed. Commoner, kneel before me. *(He does. To* NATASHA) Prince, here is the Pledge of Purity which the commoner must sign. Show it to him.

NATASHA *takes* PERCY *the pledge.*

PERCY *(quietly):* What is this?

NATASHA: Read it.

PERCY *(reads):* It's a legal contract!

NATASHA: Yes.

PERCY *(reads):* What?! You want me to surrender half of what I've got left from the land deal?

ALICE: Read on.

PERCY: But Alice –

ALICE: Read.

PERCY *(reads):* And give it to a newspaper for womens' rights?

NATASHA: Yes.

PERCY: But Alice, how can we get married? How can I start my own paper? How can we move to British Columbia? I did this for you!

ALICE: If you still love me, sign!

PERCY *signs with a pen provided by* NATASHA.

ALICE *(to* PERCY): Thank you. *(To* ALL) Dearly beloved, now that the commoner has signed the Pledge of Purity, I advise all present that he has confessed his transgressions. I will now seek a blessing for him. *(Holds out hands in blessing.)* May your heart be opened to a knowledge of all that true love could bring you. May your mind awaken to an understanding of the price you could pay for its loss. May the mercy of forgiveness fall upon you.

PERCY: Does this mean you forgive me?

ALICE: Yes. But it doesn't mean I'm going to marry you.

PERCY: It doesn't?!

ALICE: No.

ANYA: And so our play draws to a close!

ANYA *beckons the* PIANO PLAYER *to play the reprise of "Magic Reversals Waltz." He begins, and the* WOMEN *start to sing.*

WOMEN:

Oh Magic (oh Magic) Reversals
Nothing is quite what it seems
(What it seems to be)
Magic (oh Magic) Reversals

RAKER *(stepping forward at last, somewhere in mid-song):* Stop that music! Stop! *(The* PIANO PLAYER *stops in confusion.)* Stop the play! This isn't how it's supposed to work out!

ALICE: Just a minute, Father. Mr. Shrike?

SHRIKE: Your Grace? I mean, Miss Raker?

ALICE: Is your generous offer to travel to Winnipeg with you in your special coach still open?

SHRIKE *(not believing his fortune):* You want to come with me to Winnipeg?! In my own special coach?! *(Exulting.)* Of course...Alice. Whenever you wish.

PERCY: Alice, what are you doing?

ALICE: Then I accept your offer, Mr. Shrike.

RAKER: You want to go with Shrike now? But I thought –

PERCY: Alice!

SHRIKE *(a paroxysm of lust):* She accepts! She accepts!

ALICE: Yes. I do accept...a ride. My father and I will travel with you to Winnipeg...where I will enter University –

RAKER, SHRIKE *&* PERCY: University?!

ALICE: And board with Mrs. McClung!

MEN: With Mrs. McClung!?

ALICE: I'm going to be a lawyer! I want to fight for women's rights!

JEAN: Good girl! We need at least one decent lawyer in this city!

RAKER: Now just a minute. I'm not having my daughter become a lawyer. You told me you wanted to marry Percy, and you're going to marry Percy!

ANYA *(stepping forward):* No, Sidney, she isn't.

RAKER *(stopped in his tracks):* Anya....

OTHERS: Sidney?

ANYA *(to audience):* My friends.

RAKER: Anya...no!

ANYA: My friends! I have something to say that I have wanted to say for a long time.

RAKER: No, not that!

ANYA: Yes, Sidney, it is more than time that everyone knew.

RAKER: No, please, not in front of everybody.

NATASHA: Knew what, mother?

ANYA: Everyone knows that Mayor Raker had a wife here in Regina who died giving birth to this child, Alice.

ALL: Yes.

ANYA: What everyone does not know is that some years ago in Toronto, when I was still Anya Berekowski –

PERCY, INK & SHRIKE: Berekowski?!

JEAN & NELLIE: Berekowski is a very fine Ukrainian name!

ANYA: As I was saying...some years ago in Toronto, Mr. Raker and I met, and I became the first Mrs. Raker.

Gasps of amazement.

ANYA: Yes. And we had a child.

More gasps of amazement. "A child!" etc.

ANYA: Natasha...that child was you!

NATASHA: Me!!!?

OTHERS: Her!!?

ANYA: Soon after your birth, we found we couldn't get along and –

ALICE *&* NATASHA: Then we're –

ANYA: Yes.

ALICE *&* NATASHA: Sisters!!!!!

INK *(to* SHRIKE) *&* JEAN *(to* NELLIE): They're sisters!!

> NATASHA *and* ALICE *fall into each other's arms.* JEAN *and* NELLIE *applaud and cheer.*

ALICE: Natasha!

NATASHA: Alice! I've always wanted a sister!

ALICE *(turns to* ANYA, *hugs her):* And I've always wanted a mother!

PERCY *(an idea. Looks at* NATASHA): Then you're the Mayor's daughter too.

RAKER: Anya?

ANYA: Yes, Sidney?

RAKER: Do you think we....

ANYA: You'd have to change so many of your dreadful ways.

RAKER: I might give it a try.

ANYA: I don't know, Sidney.

INK *(distraught):* It isn't fair! At the end, we were supposed to steal their weapons and take over. Then the men would be in control again and things would be the way they're supposed to be! And then *we* would fight for power –

SHRIKE: And you would have died a terrible death on the blade of a sword.

INK: A terrible death!!

SHRIKE: So maybe you like this ending better, eh, Mr. Ink?

INK: Yes, I guess I do.

SHRIKE: You didn't have to pretend to lose your life, you only had to really lose half of your money!

INK: Oh!! That's right too!

SHRIKE: You stupid fool! (INK *takes a consoling drink.)*

PERCY: Excuse me, Mr. Mayor, but you promised me I could marry your daughter.

RAKER: Yes, I did.

PERCY: Well I want to hold you to your promise.

RAKER: But how – ?

PERCY *(to* NATASHA): I'm truly sorry for what happened. I swear to you I'll never touch Demon Drink again. Will you forgive me? Will you marry me?

NATASHA *(to* ANYA): Mother, what do you think? *(To* ALICE.) Sister, can I believe him?

ANYA & ALICE: Well...I think so.

NATASHA: All right. *(Pause.)* Mr. Thistle.

PERCY: Percy?

NATASHA: Percy. *(Pulls out contract.)* But you better read this marriage contract first!

PERCY: Another contract?! *(Laughs. Realizes.)* You had all this planned!

ALICE: "Magic Reversals."

PERCY *(to* NATASHA): You better still be in charge of making saskatoon pie!

NATASHA *(laughs):* I will be!

PERCY: Well then, we better move back to Saskatoon where there's the biggest and juiciest berries you'll ever see. And then...*(Starts singing "Saskatoon Pie.")*

Wouldn't you like to pick berries with me

In the warm sunshine, down in the ravines

PERCY & NATASHA:

Baskets of saskatoons, purple and sweet
And we'll make pie out of what we don't eat!

Oh, oh, saskatoon pie!
I'll give you a piece of my saskatoon pie!
(You'll give me a piece of your saskatoon pie!)

ANYA *stands with* RAKER, INK *with* JEAN, *and* ALICE *and* NELLIE *on either side of* SHRIKE.

WOMEN:

All of the bushes are heavy and sway
With berries ripe in the heat of the day
They'll fall in our hands, burst on our tongues
Filling our mouths full of juice from the sun

ALL:

Oh, oh, saskatoon pie!
We'll share a piece of sweet saskatoon pie!

Or down on the bank of the river we'll lie
Through dancing leaves watch clouds drifting by
Ripples of water will carry our dream
Into a future that flows like the stream

Oh-oh-oh-oh, saskatoon pie!
Oh-oh-oh-oh, saskatoon pie!
Can't you just taste that sweet saskatoon pie?
Can't you just taste that sweet saskatoon pie?

END OF PLAY

FLORENCE BEAN JAMES

In 1954 Florence Bean James rides six hours on a train. It is thirty degrees below zero. Mrs. James, at sixty-one, is ready to start a new career. She is going to coach an amateur drama group in rural Saskatchewan. The group, after a few sessions, has to stop rehearsals because of unusually warm weather. The actors have to drive their combines. The actors have to harvest grain.

"That was a waste," commented one Seattle artist reflecting on Florence's immigration to Canada and away from her famed Seattle Repertory Playhouse. Why a waste, I asked. Well, said the artist, Florence was capable of the most finished kind of theatre work. In Saskatchewan she was working with totally untrained people.

Mrs. James, however, did not consider her work in Saskatchewan a waste. She worked with amateur groups, professional groups, farmers' co-ops, United Church Women, Ken Mitchell, Jean Freeman, Shirley Douglas, Sue Kramer, Mary Ellen Burgess, Ken Kramer, W.O. Mitchell, and countless others. It is not an exaggeration to say that anyone in serious Saskatchewan theatre was either taught by Florence James or taught by somebody who was.

For Mrs. James, Saskatchewan was not a waste because it provided an opportunity for what she called a "living" theatre, a theatre "by, for, and of the people." The United States would not permit her to make that contribution; during the Cold War she was blacklisted for politically relevant cultural activity. The unique living theatre that flourishes in Saskatchewan is arguably a result of our association with Florence Bean James.

She believed that you needed two things to succeed: talent and opportunity. Tommy Douglas's Co-operative Commonwealth Federation, the first socialist government in North America, had been elected in 1944. In 1948 the CCF had created the Saskatchewan Arts Board to give "the people of Saskatchewan the opportunity to participate in music, drama, visual arts, handicrafts, and other arts." This in a province without full electricity, bus service, or a decent auditorium in the capital city – in a country that did not yet have a Canada Council.

When she was past the age of sixty, Florence James was ready to grasp the new opportunity and pass it on to those with talent. She boarded trains that would take her to small town Saskatchewan whenever a group asked. "I wasn't hired weather permitting." She stayed in hotels that did not have private bathrooms or fire escapes, and worked with anyone who wanted to stage a play.

Florence said in one of her reports to the arts board during the fifties that she was "sowing seeds" and eventually there would be a "bumper harvest." Since that statement there have been lean and fat theatrical years, years of drought, depression, and abundant aesthetic richness.

The unique features of Saskatchewan theatre are reflected in the sense of artistic/social purpose passed on to us by Florence James. It is totally appropriate that Coteau Books should name this drama series for her. Florence understood that there could be no living theatre without writing, music, design, and performance growing out of the issues, the cultures, and the people of a region. Her kind of theatre spoke of history, labour, politics, racism, and deep human relationships. From her earliest teaching days at Fort San, she encouraged and commissioned the playwrights of the region, because for her local writing was the foundation of a living, growing, rooted theatre.

The result of the opportunities Florence Bean James gave to us are evident in this series of scripts. It's a bumper harvest.

RITA SHELTON DEVERELL
Toronto

GEOFFREY URSELL

GEOFFREY URSELL IS AN AWARD-WINNING WRITER OF DRAMA, POETRY, fiction, and songs. His first novel *Perdue*, published by Macmillian in 1984, won the prestigious *Books in Canada* First Novel Award for that year. His play "The Running of the Deer" won the 1977 Clifford E. Lee National Playwriting Award. *Saskatoon Pie!* won Persephone Theatre's 1981 National Playwriting Competition, set a theatre attendance record at Persephone in 1982, and was remounted and toured Saskatchewan in 1986 with great success.

He has also written drama for radio and television, including *The Rum-Runners of Rainbow Ravine*, a ten-part mystery-comedy for CBC Radio Saskatchewan, *Journey to a Secret Sea*, for CBC Network's "Vanishing Point," and *Distant Battles*, a one-hour television drama about the events of the rebellion/resistance of the Metis in 1885.

Trap Lines, his first book of poetry, was published by Turnstone Press in 1983, and received a Special Commendation from the Commonwealth Poetry Prize Competition. A new collection of poetry, *The Look-Out Tower*, was released by Turnstone in 1989. *Way Out West!*, a collection of short stories, was also published by Fifth House in 1989.

Geoffrey has composed songs and music for many plays by other writers, including the music for Don Kerr's *Talking Back*, about the founding of the CCF in the 1930s, produced at Twenty-Fifth Street Theatre in 1988. His songs are featured on two record albums, and his songs, poems, and stories have appeared in many Canadian periodicals and anthologies.

An editor of three anthologies of short stories, as well as many single author titles, Geoffrey has also co-edited two anthologies of writing for children for Coteau Books. Past-President of the Saskatchewan Writer's Guild and the Saskatchewan Playwrights Centre, Geoffrey has been Writer-in-Residence at the Saskatoon and Winnipeg Public Libraries, and has taught Canadian literature and creative writing at the University of Regina.

Geoffrey was born in Moose Jaw, Saskatchewan, in 1943, and grew up in various prairie cities. He received his M.A. from the University of Manitoba, and his Ph.D. from the University of London, England. He and his wife, Barbara Sapergia, both write full-time in Saskatoon.